EXOTIC MASSAGE
for Lovers

EXOTIC MASSAGE
for Lovers

Timothy Freke

Massage Consultant: Yvette Mayo

Photography by Alistair Hughes, Howard Allman
and Barry Chandler

STERLING PUBLISHING CO., INC.
New York

This book is dedicated to the omnipresent power of love.

ADVICE TO THE READER

Published 1996 by Sterling Publishing Company, Inc.
387 Park Avenue South, New York, N.Y. 10016
Originally published 1996 in Great Britain
by Boxtree Limited, Broadwall House, 21 Broadwall, London SE1 9PL
Text copyright © Timothy Freke 1996
Photographs copyright © Vyner Street Studios 1996
Illustrations copyright © Alan McGowan 1996
This edition copyright © Eddison Sadd Editions 1996
Distributed in Canada by Sterling Publishing
c/o Canadian Manda Group, One Atlantic Avenue, Suite 105
Toronto, Ontario, Canada M6K 3E7

Library of Congress Cataloging-in-Publication Data Available

2 4 6 8 10 9 7 5 3 1

AN EDDISON·SADD EDITION
Edited, designed and produced by
Eddison Sadd Editions Limited
St Chad's House
148 King's Cross Road
London WC1X 9DH

Phototypeset in Bernhard Modern using QuarkXPress on Apple Macintosh
Printed in Hong Kong

Sterling ISBN 0-8069-6170-8

Contents

Celebrating the Senses

The senses are our means of connecting our private inner world of thoughts, feelings and imagination with the shared world which we see, hear, smell, taste and touch. Every moment of every day, our senses are alert to the wealth of information reaching them. In our stressful modern society, this can feel less like bathing in sublime sensation, and more like drowning under an ever rising tide of unwelcome stimulation – which bombards us from all directions.

In the midst of busy lives, it is important to make the time to remember that the senses are the source of all physical pleasure, and to resensitise ourselves to the rich enjoyment that they can bring. Sharing sensual massage with your lover is a particularly rewarding way to awaken the natural delights of the senses. Not only can it ease away the cares of life, helping to relax both body and mind; it can also enhance and transform your love-making, opening up new horizons of sexual gratification and emotional connection. In this age of AIDS, it also offers a fulfilling and safe way to enjoy physical intimacy, without intercourse.

Sensual massage is easy. The carefully selected techniques in this book are quick to learn and simple to perform, so that you and your lover can let go and enjoy the experience. Your skin, and an enjoyment of touching and being touched, are all you need to give or receive a sensual massage (although, of course, if you have a health problem or are pregnant it may be advisable to seek medical advice first). By helping relaxation, massage can improve general health and promote a feeling of well-being, but the techniques presented here are, first and foremost, about enjoying intimate pleasure with your lover.

Intimate Touching

Touching is a powerful form of communication, and one which is surrounded, in most societies, by strictly observed taboos. We may shake a stranger by the hand, and embrace a friend or member of our family, but usually only a lover has access to our more private and most sensitive parts. Despite the fact that these areas are so pleasurably responsive to touch, we reserve them for someone with whom we have a sexual relationship. Withholding physical intimacy from all but a lover is one way of making that relationship special, and creating a powerful emotional bond.

When such a relationship is developing, a lover gradually allows his or her partner to touch places of overpowering sensuality. Often, however, once this 'courting ritual' has been performed, love-play becomes focused on these overtly sexual areas. This familiarity is comforting and can be sexually exciting, but it sometimes blinds us to the enjoyment offered by other parts of the body. It may also prevent a natural build-up of desire and sensitivity, so that we no longer have the opportunity to become as powerfully sexually aroused. Sharing sensual massage is a perfect way to recover and develop this natural process of stimulation, teasing and arousal.

To help you and your lover in this process,

this book traces the natural progression towards greater intimacy, taking you, chapter by chapter, on a guided journey of sensual discovery. Starting with relaxation and awakening the responses to subtle touch, there are clear 'hands-on' instructions and stimulating step-by-step photographs explaining massage techniques for the whole body: the back, feet, head, buttocks, belly, breasts, and, finally, the genitals. Such loving attention is a powerful part of foreplay, leading naturally to a state of deep sexual receptivity, and allowing a total erotic experience of manual, oral and penetrative love-making.

Many of us, especially men, are often 'out of touch' with our feelings and sensuality. This can lead to love-making becoming mechanical and colourless. Sensual massage is about delighting in simple enjoyment of the body. It can reorientate sexuality, changing it from a brief rush to orgasm, into something more like a slow luxurious bath in an ocean of pleasure. The destination is not orgasm, because there is no destination. Enjoying the journey itself is the goal. And an orgasm arrived at through such a journey is richer and more satisfying, as a result of diving deeply into the realm of the senses.

Ancient Sensual Wisdom

It is only over the last few decades that the West has begun to explore the eastern art of sexual ecstasy, yet, for centuries, Taoist philosophy from China and Tantric religious traditions from India have encouraged an uninhibited celebration of the senses. As early as 3,000 years before Christ, there was reference to massage in a Chinese treatise called *Nei Ching*, credited to the mythical Yellow Emperor Huang-Ti. The Indian books of the *Ayur Veda*, written about 1,000 years later, also extol its virtues. Over the follow-ing millennia, many traditions exploring the sensual arts flourished in the East. In the following pages this profound understanding of erotic pleasure is introduced to modern lovers in a fresh and approachable way.

Tantra and Taoism teach that, during sensual massage, maximum arousal is reached, not only through the position of the hands, but also through the focus of our attention. The massage techniques in this book are accompanied by simple suggestions, based on this ancient wisdom, which help you to use the power of the mind to deepen and enhance the pleasure of the body. These straightforward easy-to-practise techniques can open up a new level of sexual enjoyment. They are not esoteric or other-worldly practices. They are direct ways of exploring fully the delights of love-making.

Using this Book

Sensual massage is an art, like playing a musical instrument. We may easily pick up an enjoyable melody, but it takes time and repetition to achieve beautiful phrasing and a smooth pleasing rhythm. However, the process of mastering sensual massage is a joy in itself. You don't have to practise all of the techniques immediately, neither do you have to use them every time. Imagine them as a repertoire, to be explored with your lover.

At first, the idea of using the mind as well as the hands for massage may seem a little strange. If this is the case, choose the techniques that you find the most interesting and appealing; play with them, and save the others for a different time. Throughout the ages, these techniques have brought to ordinary people – like you and me – an enhanced physical enjoyment and deeper emotional and spiritual intimacy.

CHAPTER ONE

The Pleasure Chamber

Decorate the pleasure chamber
with beautiful pictures and fine objects,
upon which the eye may dwell with delight.

Scatter some musical instruments and refreshments,
rosewater, essences, fans,
books containing amorous songs
and illustrations of love-postures.

Let splendid wall lights gleam,
reflected by wide mirrors,
while both man and woman having no reserve or false shame,
give themselves up in complete nakedness
to their unrestrained passions
upon a fine bed, ornate with many useful pillows
and covered with a canopy.

Sprinkle the sheets with flowers and scent,
and let sweet incense be burned.
Here, the lovers may enjoy each other
in ease and comfort,
gratifying each other's every wish and whim.

Ananga Ranga

Creating a Pleasure Chamber

In the Ancient East, erotic sensual delights were enjoyed in a special pleasure chamber, whereas, today, we would normally make love in the bedroom. Try changing the name of this room, so that, rather than being a bedroom where you make love, it becomes a pleasure chamber where you also sleep.

Whatever the choice of room, fill your pleasure chamber with sensuality; make it sumptuous, with attractive pictures and beautiful objects. You may like to prepare the pleasure chamber for your lover as a surprise, but it is fun to create it together. Be imaginative! Bring fruits and wine to eat and drink. Create a seductive and sexy atmosphere; dim the lights or use a coloured bulb; light candles and play soothing, erotic music. Burn incense or essential oils to fill the room with a sweet bewitching fragrance. If the pleasure chamber is special and intimate, your love-play is more likely to have the same qualities.

When you meet your lover in the pleasure chamber, allow yourself to let go of the cares and worries of the day. Make sure you will not be disturbed; unplug the phone. This is a time to step out of the world of plans and work, and into the fullness of the present moment. Abandon yourself to the immediate sensory experiences; the aroma of essential oils, the textures of the music, and the smooth caresses of caring hands on soft skin.

The whole body is covered in pleasure receptors, all of which can be stimulated to give erotic enjoyment. Clothes place a physical barrier between you and your lover, so try the following techniques with both of you naked. This will make you feel free and open, and perhaps a little vulnerable, which can be exciting. You may like to share a luxurious bath together before you massage each other. Try scenting the water with fragrant essential oils, such as ylang ylang, lavender, jasmine, patchouli or sandalwood.

Being openly naked is not something which everyone finds easy. Don't push yourself or your lover to do anything that either of you doesn't feel comfortable about. If you don't want to be naked, just wear something light and loose which allows as much sensitivity to touch as possible. Make sure the room is at a comfortable temperature; consider using an electric blanket as an under blanket to keep your lover warm during the massage. Think about this before you start; it is a real passion-killer to have to break off in the middle of a massage to switch on a heater.

Body Language

Decide which one of you is going to give the massage, and which one is to receive. You may both want to give a massage, one after the other, or you may want to take it in turns on different occasions. The pleasure of giving can be just as great as the pleasure of receiving. By totally focusing attention on your lover's body, you will be able to share the pleasure, achieving a deeper emotional bond together. Whether giving or receiving massage, you are partaking in a special kind of intimate conversation, spoken in body-language.

As you perform the simple massage techniques of this chapter, be aware of what your lover's body is telling you. Your partner may, of course, respond in words: 'That feels good,' or, 'Do that again.' Sometimes, however, just as much can be said with a sigh or heavy breathing; subtle movements of the body or the tensing and relaxing of muscles. Bodies speak a language all of their own and such non-verbal messages communicate on a very deep level.

If you can feel where your lover wants you to explore next, it is important to respond. This builds up a flow of trust and communication. Every person's tolerance to pleasure is different. Watch the face, and feel the body under your fingertips. Listen to your lover's body language, so that you can tell when he or she wants you to move on, and when a movement is enjoyable.

Giving a massage is a way of saying 'I love you' through body language, without needing to use words. Be aware of your feelings of care for and attraction towards your lover. Imagine that, instead of speaking these thoughts, you are expressing them with your hands, and performing a kind of magic with your mind. Such ideas can subtly affect the quality of your touch and, if receptive, your lover will feel the difference.

If you are being massaged, focus completely on your lover's touch. The more involved you become, the stronger will be the feelings of relaxation and arousal. Sense the pleasure that your partner is giving. How does it feel? What is being said to you? Hold on to your feelings of love and gratitude and, instead of speaking, convey them using the natural and innate language of the body. Guide your partner in the ways which give you maximum enjoyment.

It is often said that people don't communicate enough. Lovers, in particular, often get tangled up in verbal misunderstandings, and find themselves unable to share their deepest feelings. Here is a simple way to allow a profound and sensual flow of communication, from body to body.

Harmonizing

In the traditions of the ancient East, sensual massage is about you and your lover finding a magical intimate togetherness where it feels as if you have merged, to become one. In the traditions of the East, it is recommended that lovers take a few minutes to harmonize their moods and 'energies' before beginning massage. This first technique will help you 'tune-in'. Ask your lover to lie face down in a relaxed and comfortable position.

Rub your palms together vigorously, to warm them and avoid giving a cold and unpleasant shock. In Taoism and Tantra we are told that the physical body is surrounded by a subtle 'energy-body' or 'aura'. Briskly rubbing the hands together invigorates this energy and focuses it in the hands, promoting a more stimulating massage.

Kneel comfortably to the left of your partner. Gently place the palm of your right hand on the bottom of your partner's spine, and the palm of your left hand on the top of the spine at the base of the neck (right). Close your eyes and use your mind to tune-in to your partner. Be aware of his or her feelings, and send loving thoughts through the palms of your hands.

The 'subtle energies' of the body can be stimulated and controlled by using the power of the mind. Imagine a flowing energy passing down your left arm, through your left palm, down your lover's spine, into your right palm and up your right arm, forming a circle which unites the two of you. Ask your partner to help by also visualizing this flow of energy.

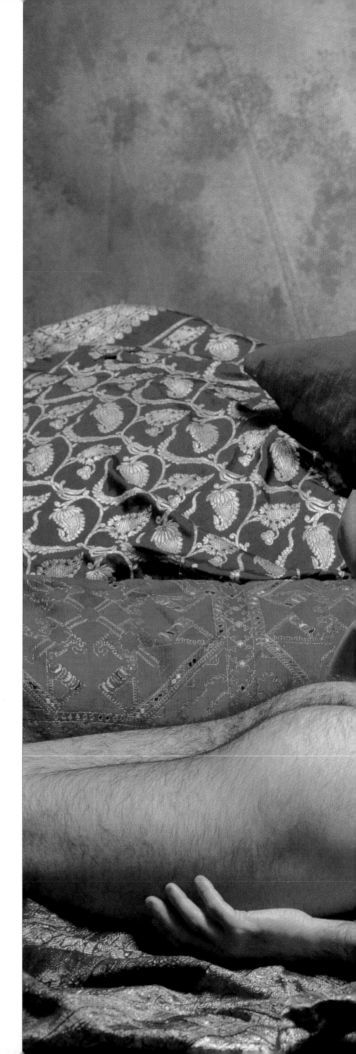

Removing Negative Energy

Just like the body, the aura gets dirty and needs cleaning of the 'negative energies' picked up each day from the world around us, and created by our own negative thoughts and feelings. When you feel ready, place your hands softly on the back of your partner's head (right). With an extremely light touch, sweep your hands down your lover's body. Imagine that you are brushing away all the tension and negative energy in his or her aura, leaving it clean and sensitive.

Sweep down the back...

... and legs and off at the feet.

Do this a few times, expanding the sweep to include the whole back and both arms. End each sweep by removing your hands and flicking them lightly into empty space to one side, as if shaking off droplets of water, to remove any negative energy that you may have picked up.

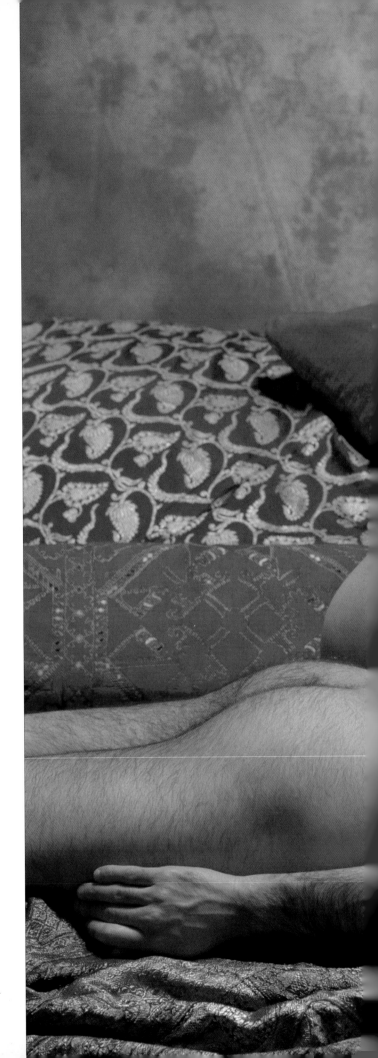

Relax and Prepare for Pleasure

Begin by awakening your lover to your touch. Gently and very slowly, stroke his or her back with the ends of your fingertips. In this feathering technique, the pressure should be as light as a gliding feather. If your partner finds this ticklish, slightly increase the pressure until it is comfortable. Gradually move your fingertips around the whole body. This pleasantly teasing stimulation awakens the nerve endings, sending a signal to the brain to relax and prepare for pleasure.

There are no right and wrong ways in sensual massage. All that matters is finding what you and your partner enjoy. Follow your intuitive feelings about where your hands should go next. Watch the reactions carefully, and respond in the way you feel is appropriate, bathing your lover in the exquisite feeling of caring hands on sensitive skin. If your hair is long enough, trail it softly across your lover's body to give a water-like sensation (left). If you lower and raise the head this can feel like gentle rising and falling waves.

You may also like to try scratching lightly with your nails (above). This should be very soft so that it does not hurt, but gives a pleasantly abrasive stimulation. Make sure your nails have no sharp edges. Try alternating between feathering and scratching, so that your lover is never sure which to expect.

Exotic Ways to Wake the Senses

Soft fabrics like silk, velvet and soft fur are also deliciously sensual when passed lightly over the body (right). Find a silk scarf and waft it over your lover, like a gentle breeze. Or place it under the palm of your hand and, using hardly any pressure, glide it provocatively over the skin. Because there is so little resistance, this can be done quite quickly, as well as slowly. Vary the tempo to surprise and delight your partner.

An even more erotic way of preparing the body for the pleasure of massage is to pass your breasts lightly across your lover's body (above), tantalizing him with the touch of your nipples and soft flesh.

Try using your lips and tongue in the same way, as softly as possible. Gently pull your relaxed bottom lip over your partner's skin (stopping from time to time to lick your lips to keep them moist). Use your tongue; tickle your lover with small, quick movements of the tip, then long luxurious strokes of the whole tongue. Stop occasionally to blow softly where you have been kissing (above).

CHAPTER TWO

Easing and Teasing

Woman is like a fruit
which will not yield its sweetness
until you rub it between your hands.
Look at the basil plant –
if you do not rub it warm with your fingers,
it will not emit any scent.

Do you not know that the amber,
unless it be handled and warmed,
keeps hidden within its pores
the aroma contained in it.

It is the same with woman.
If you do not animate her with your toying,
intermixed with kissing,
nibbling and touching,
you will not obtain from her what you are wishing;
you will feel no enjoyment when you share her couch,
and you will waken in her heart
neither inclination, nor affection,
nor love for you.
All her qualities will remain hidden.

Shaykh Nefzawi,
The Perfumed Garden

Breath Awareness

Much of the ancient wisdom of Taoism and Tantra points towards the power of the simple things in life; the obvious things, which we so often overlook. Some Buddhists, for example, spend sixteen hours a day, for months on end, simply paying attention to their breath as it goes in and out! Strange as this may seem, they find that this gives a deep insight into the nature of life, and can lead to a profoundly pleasurable experience.

As you massage your lover, or while being massaged, become aware of the sensation of breathing. This may push away the cares of the day, the concerns of past and future, and bring a fuller enjoyment of the present moment. Breathing is ever present, from the moment of birth. Just be aware of it rising and falling. Don't try to force other thoughts away; and don't worry if your mind constantly wanders. Return to your breathing, whenever you remember – and relax.

Imagine that your mind is like a clear blue sky, and your thoughts are like passing clouds. Concentrate not on the clouds but on the spacious emptiness in which they float. Focusing on your breath will help you ignore the chatter of thoughts which clutters the mind. Just as tea leaves settle slowly to the bottom of a cup when it is not being stirred; so the thoughts in your mind will settle into a deep receptive peace, as long as you don't pay them too much attention.

Breathing in Unison

Gradually let your breathing rhythm synchronize with that of your lover, so that you both breathe in and out at the same time. Don't force this; if the two lung capacities are very different, one of you may become short of breath. However, if breathing in unison arises easily and naturally, it is a wonderful technique for creating a deep sense of togetherness.

Be aware that the two of you are breathing the same air. Not only are you intimately connected by the power of touch, you are also linked by the invisible connection of the air that you both breathe. While exhaling, imagine the love and attraction that you feel is actually passing from you to your lover.

Easing and Teasing

Focusing on the simple sensation of breathing is used in Tantra and Taoism to aid relaxation and acceptance, a prerequisite for heightening sensual pleasure. The massage techniques in this chapter concentrate on helping the body to let go. They will ease the tension in the back and neck, where we store a lot of stress, but, though the focus is on 'easing' for the moment, a little 'teasing' adds an enjoyable erotic undercurrent.

While massaging, occasionally allow your hair or breasts to touch your lover, making him or her aware of your adjacent naked body. Add a soft kiss on the back, just once, between hand strokes. Press your thighs provocatively against your lover's, casually, apparently unconsciously. Such teasing starts the slow build of sexual energy, from the very first moment. Remember though, that this is only teasing; if overdone, you might well cause too much arousal prematurely, and lose patience with the massage!

Using Massage Oil

For the following massage techniques, it is important that hands slide easily over skin. A little oil will lubricate the body, making it smooth and soft. Place a few drops of oil on your hand. Gently rub both hands together, and smooth the oil onto your lover's skin. Repeat this whenever necessary. While oiling your hands, try to maintain some physical contact with your partner, as the sudden feeling of absence can break the flow; perhaps, rest the back of a hand on your lover's body, or keep contact with a leg, or arm. Generally, throughout the whole massage session, try to keep 'in touch'.

Don't use hand cream or body lotion, as this is too easily absorbed by the skin; it is better to purchase specially prepared massage oils, or create your own using fragrant essential oils. Choose a base oil; sweet almond, walnut or olive oil are especially good for sensual massage. For every 10 ml of base oil, add 3–6 drops of fragrant essential oil.

The aromas of some essential oils, such as ylang ylang, jasmine, clary sage and patchouli, are said to be aphrodisiacs. Oil of orange blossom (better known as neroli, extracted from the white blossoms of the bitter orange); rose otto (the most expensive of oils – it takes thirty roses to make one drop); and sandalwood (mentioned in ancient *Vedic* writings of the fifth century BC) blend well together to make a powerful concoction. Essential oils are also good for you; rose otto, for instance, is excellent for rejuvenating dry skin. Experiment with different fragrances, to see which ones are most stimulating for you and your partner.

Easing the Back

Kneel alongside or astride your lover's buttocks, with most of your weight resting on your knees. This can be a more erotic position, because your partner will feel the movement of your thighs and genitals every time you stretch forward and move back (make sure your lover finds this comfortable). Place both palms on the small of your lover's back, on either side of the spine, with fingers pointing up towards the head (left). Using flat palms, sweep up either side of your lover's spine. Apply gentle pressure, using your full weight and taking plenty of time.

Sweep across the top of the shoulders...

...and down the sides of the body, bringing your hands together again, at the base of your lover's spine. Repeat this circular sequence, slowly and sensually.

Sensual Strokes for the Back

Place your hands on your lover's shoulder blades, at the top, so the thumbs fall either side of the top of the spine. Use the thumbs to knead the muscles, as if kneading dough; applying pressure and then releasing (right). The shoulders are a major store house of stress. Press hard enough to move the muscle, but not so hard that it hurts. Move slowly out around the top of the shoulder blades. You are in an ideal position while doing this to kiss the hair, or the nape of the neck, casually, in passing.

Knead the soft flesh on the side of the belly in the same way, but using less pressure (right).

With your palms downwards, point the fingers of both hands together to form an arrow shape, catching a little of the skin of your lover's back between your hands (right).

Then turn your hands over, so that, as the palms come together, your lover's skin slips out from between your fingers (right). This is known as butterfly massage. Repeat all over the back.

Soothing Stress Away

Place a thumb on one side of your lover's neck, with the fingers on the other side (left). Knead the neck with thumb and fingers, applying pressure and then releasing, to loosen the accumulated tension. A woman could occasionally let her breasts brush delicately across her lover's back while performing this massage.

With gentle pressure, follow the contours of the base of your lover's skull with your thumbs, applying pressure and then releasing.

'If lovers spend time playing with and caressing each other, then their ecstasy and confidence increases. Love-play enhances pleasure.'

Kama Sutra

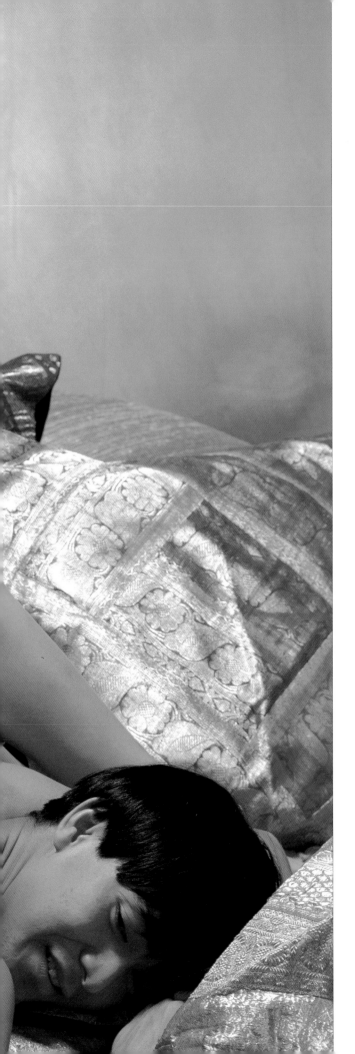

Spine Sensations

Place both thumbs, nail to nail, on the left side of the base of your lover's spine. Apply pressure with the thumbs, and then release. Work slowly up the left side of your lover's spine in this way. When you reach the top, remove hands and repeat on the right side of the spine (left and below).

Place your thumbs, as before, on the left of the base of your lover's spine. Applying pressure, slide them about 20 cm (8 in) up the spine (below).

Lift your hands away, and circle back about 10 cm (4 in). Place your thumbs as before and repeat the upward pressure against the spine. Work your way up your lover's back in this 'two steps forward, one step back' fashion, until you reach the top of the spine. Repeat on the right side of the spine.

CHAPTER THREE

Natural Pleasures

How beautiful are thy feet with shoes.
The joints of thy thighs are like jewels.
The work of the hands of a cunning workman.

Thy navel is like a round goblet,
which wanteth not liquor:
Thy belly is like an heap of wheat,
set about with lilies.

Thy two breasts are like two young roses
– that are twins.

Thy neck is as a tower of ivory.
Thine eyes like the fishpools of Heshbon.
Thy lips drop as the honeycomb,
honey and milk are under thy tongue.

How fair, how pleasant art thou, O love,
for delights!

Song of Solomon

Song of the Senses

King Solomon is said to have had 700 wives and 300 concubines! When you read his *Song of Songs* (an extract opens this chapter) you can see why. This beautiful erotic poetry is part of the Holy Bible! Obviously, in Old Testament times, the people of the Middle East must have delighted in singing the songs of the senses.

The ancient West was also not without an appreciation of the sensual arts. Among the Greeks and Romans, famous men such as Homer, Herodotus, Hippocrates, Socrates, Plato, Julius Caesar, and Pliny, all praised the power of massage. Tantric sexual practices reached the West from India around 2,000 BC, through the ecstatic cult of the god Dionysus, which celebrated the sanctity of sensuality; but the pleasures of the flesh came to be seen increasingly as evil temptations, rather than wonders of God's creation, and massage increasingly fell into disrepute. By the Middle Ages, it was often seen as an unhealthy indulgence to be avoided by the righteous.

For many eastern traditions, however, the enjoyment of the senses remained a healthy, even holy, part of life. The body was seen as a manifestation of Mother Nature, to be worshipped and appreciated. According to these teachings, touch not only satisfies the desires of the flesh, it is also food for the soul. We are all more than just a body; we are also spiritual beings. Tender caresses are emotionally reassuring as well as physically stimulating.

Such intimacy is important: it frees us from the isolation of our own separate inner world and connects us to another human being. In Tantra and Taoism, the sensual arts involve body, mind and soul, making enjoyment more complete and therefore more fulfilling.

Taoism, the Natural Way

The Chinese philosophy of Taoism puts particular emphasis on enjoying the naturalness of life; its essence is sometimes simply expressed in the phrase 'go with the flow'. Taoism teaches us not to struggle too much or try too hard. The *Tao* is the natural way: to follow this way is to live in harmony with the natural ebb and flow of life. Fighting the currents is difficult, like trying to swim against the tide or in a rushing river; but, if we trust the river and consciously let it carry us, then life becomes an enjoyable journey to the great sea of wisdom, which is our destination.

Taoism encourages an uninhibited natural spontaneity. A Taoist master was once asked, 'What is the secret of enlightenment?' He replied, 'When tired, sleep and when hungry, eat'. We might add, 'When playful, enjoy yourself'. Bring this quality of naturalness to your love-making. Respond to the intuitions and feelings of the moment. Trust yourself. Make your love-play a natural celebration of being alive.

Many of the so-called 'spiritual' techniques of the East are about a simple reawakening of our appreciation of life; recapturing the freshness and excitement of youth, but with the wisdom and consciousness of age. We are surrounded by the mystery of life, but as we get older we often become dulled to it, thereby missing the magic. We take so much for granted. Think for a moment about the miracle of your lover's body. It can see, hear, taste, smell and feel; and, by some alchemy of the soul, your lover has the ability to enjoy these sensations – perhaps the greatest miracle of all.

The Power of Appreciation

We all have a natural drive towards feeling good, which could be seen as the underlying motivation for everything we do. But, we also need to feel appreciated, which helps us with the greatest challenge; loving and appreciating ourselves.

A powerful technique for deepening emotional intimacy is to pay compliments to your lover. Most people do this spontaneously, especially in the early days of a relationship, but later on we forget its importance. Take the opportunity, during massage to shower your partner with appreciation, as Solomon does in the *Song of Songs*.

If you find this difficult, just focus on a part of your lover's body which you find especially attractive. You might say, for example: 'You have a beautiful neck', 'I love the curves of your back', or, 'To me, you are the most special person in the world'. Include compliments on your partner's personality, such as: 'I really like your sense of fun', 'I appreciate your honesty', or, 'Being with you makes me feel good'.

Make an enjoyable game of taking turns to make appreciative comments about each other. Often it can be more difficult to accept than to give compliments. If you are embarrassed or shy, don't worry, just relax. Many of us are so used to feeling put down, or putting ourselves down, that it takes a little time to get used to being appreciated. Being made to feel lovable helps us to love more easily, for if we cannot love ourselves, we cannot truly love others. Sharing compliments can give us the confidence to love and accept what we are, and so love and accept others.

Gentle Pressure on Soft Flesh

Touching and playing with the buttocks can be intensely arousing. Kneel over your lover's legs, taking most of the weight on your knees and shins. Place the bottom of your palms on the top of your partner's thighs and push slowly upwards over the soft flesh of the buttocks. Start at the sides of the buttocks and repeat this movement, moving progressively inwards.

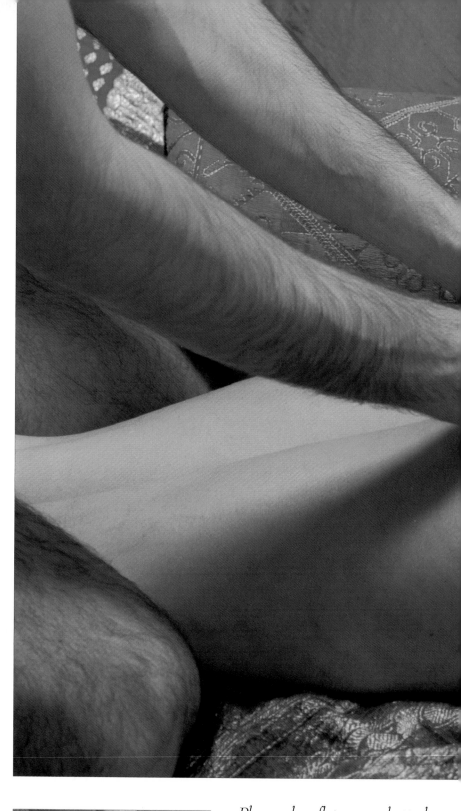

Form one of your hands into a fist and press it, knuckles down, onto your lover's buttocks (right). Apply gentle pressure with the weight of your body and then release the pressure, slowly rotating the fist around the whole area.

Place palms flat on one buttock, thumbs near the crease and fingers pointing outwards. Knead with fingers and thumbs (right), moving slowly up to the base of the spine and then back to near the thigh. Repeat with the other buttock.

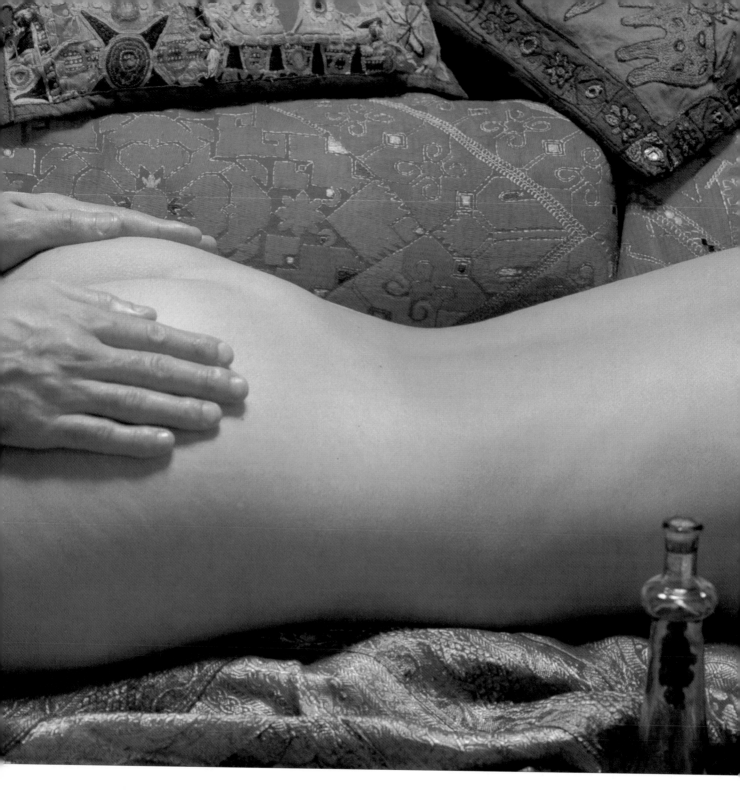

Place one palm at the top of one buttock, near the base of the spine. Stroke your hand softly along the inside of the buttock (right), and down the inside of the thighs. Repeat immediately with your other palm on the inside of the other buttock.

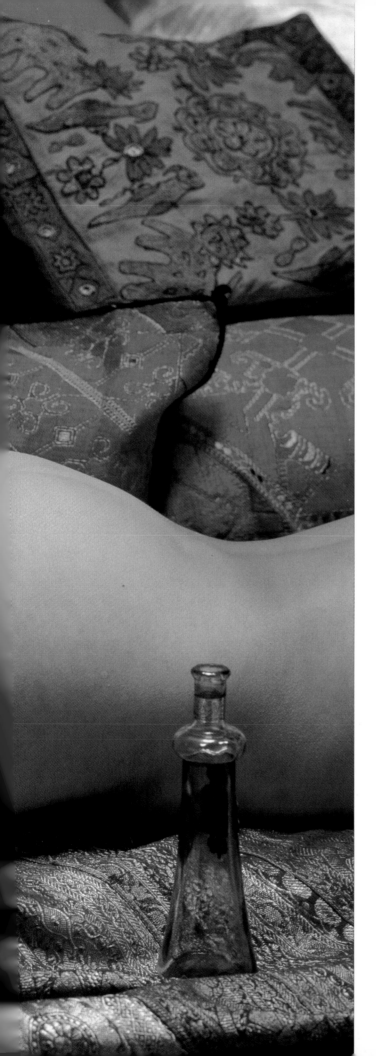

Deep Touch

Kneel alongside your lover's legs. Place your palms on top of one leg, with thumbs on one side and fingers on the other. Starting at the top of the thigh, gently knead the soft muscles of the back of the leg (left). Work your way slowly down the leg, to the bottom of the calf. Then massage back up the leg. The inside of the knee is sensitive, so stroke it softly, kissing it and then blowing gently.

Place both hands flat on top of your lover's thigh or calf. Gently, but firmly, twist your hands in opposite directions (above). Release and repeat, reversing the direction of the twist. Massage the whole leg. In passing, you could kiss your lover's buttocks, or the sensitive soles of the feet.

Hold your lover's leg at the ankle, and, very slowly, lift it so that the leg bends at the knee (above). Ask your partner to relax totally, so that you take all of the weight. Move the leg gently up and down a few times. Also, try slowly circling the leg in space, first one way and then the other. Very simple movements are often extremely enjoyable, and for some people this is surprisingly pleasant. When you feel it is time, repeat the whole sequence with the other leg.

Energizing the Legs

Kneel at your lover's feet, and place both hands around one ankle, with thumbs meeting in the middle. With gentle pressure, slide the flat of your thumbs up the middle of your lover's leg, to the top of the thigh (left and below).

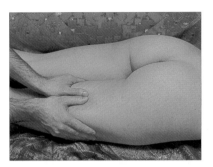

Part your hands and place the palms flat on either side of your lover's thigh.

Draw your palms towards you, sliding down to the ankle (above). Repeat this sequence a few times with each leg. The pleasing circular movement will stimulate the 'energy' channels.

'Go anoint yourself with sandalwood paste, and while the bees hum and the sun sets, we two will make love on a delightful bed strewn with flowers. I shall take much pleasure in kissing your bright red lips and caressing your body.'

Padma Purana

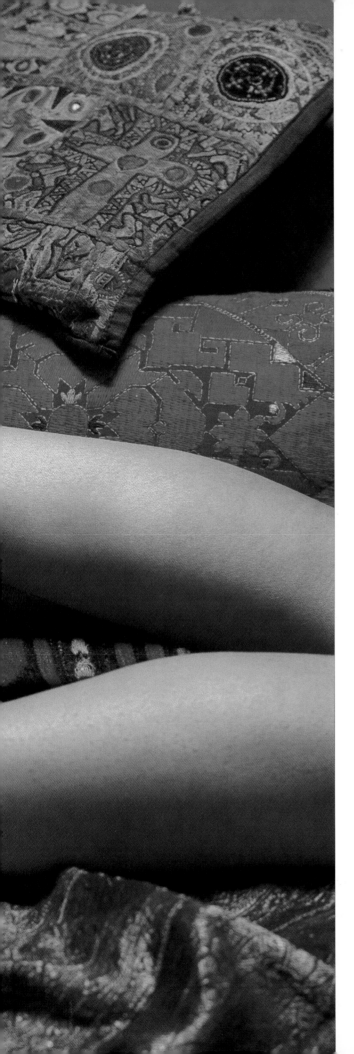

Pleasuring the Feet

The feet are deliciously sensitive, and all too often ignored as a source of sensual delight. Kneeling at your lover's feet, take one of them and place it in your lap. Place both of your thumbs in the centre of the sole, and make little circular movements, applying pressure and then releasing (left). At the same time, use your fingers to massage the other side of the foot. Slowly, explore the whole of the foot in this way, occasionally pausing to kiss and blow on the sensitive centre of the sole.

Place one hand around your lover's foot, with the thumb flat on the sole. Slowly, slide your hand off the foot, gently rolling the thumb across the sole (above). Follow immediately with your other hand, in like manner. Use your hands alternately in this way, setting up a smooth consistent rhythm.

Hold each toe in turn between your fingers and thumb (above). Massage each joint, then gently pull the toe, stretching it away from the foot. Explore the spaces between the toes with your tongue, kissing and blowing, then move on to the other foot.

CHAPTER FOUR

The Subtle Senses

Each sucks the nectar
from the other's lips,
breathing lightly – so lightly.

In those willowy hips
the passion beats.
The mocking eyes
are bright like stars.

The tiny drops of sweat
are like a hundred fragrant pearls.
The sweet full breasts
tremble.

The dew,
like a gentle stream,
reaches the heart of the peony,
and they taste the joys of love
in perfect harmony.

The Golden Lotus

Yin and Yang

Being attracted to another person, is a powerful, universal and mysterious experience. You can't make yourself feel attraction, but it's hard to ignore when it does exist! Making love is one of the most compelling and pleasurable of human activities. Each one of us is the product of this coupling. It is the foundation of the continuous unfolding of life.

All of nature reflects this coming together of masculine and feminine – the two poles of the universe which the Chinese call *Yin* and *Yang*. These two great principles are seen everywhere: dark and light, day and night, dry and moist, positive and negative, active and passive, form and content, something and nothing. Even in our number system, the idea of one is represented by '1', and the idea of nothing is represented by '0', symbols which mimic the male and female genitals.

In the Yin/Yang symbol, the black, Yin, represents the feminine, and the white, Yang, is the masculine. These two principles interpenetrate: the white contains a dot of black, and the black contains a dot of white. For Taoism and Tantra, a love affair is a journey of discovery, through which each man may experience the dot of femininity within him, and each woman may find her dot of masculinity (the psychologist Jung's *anima* and *animus*).

Yin and Yang are both contained within a circle, representing 'the whole', which the Chinese call the Tao, and others call God or Spirit. Mystics of both the East and West teach that God is love. This is the uniting principal of the universe, compelling the two poles towards union. In Tantra and Taoism, a loving relationship involves this important third party: whatever it is called, it is the power of love itself, which draws a man and woman together and contains them both.

Taoist philosophy is about finding a balance between opposites. For example, it neither puritanically condemns physical pleasures, nor hedonistically indulges them as if there were nothing more to life. It finds in them a celebration of body, mind and soul, and so defines a middle way between extreme attitudes.

The Chinese teach that Yin and Yang are not separate and distinct from each other, but mutually dependent. The Taoist sage Lao Tsu says: 'Something can be beautiful only if something else is ugly. Someone can be good only if someone else is bad. Presence and absence; short and long; high and low; before and after; gibberish and meaning; they can only exist together.'

What are often seen as irreconcilable opposites are, to the Taoists, more like the two ends of one piece of string. In the same way, man and woman are not seen in opposition, but as completely complementary. They could not exist without each other. This is obviously true because without both sexes there would be no people; but it is also true in a spiritual sense.

The ancient Greek sage Plato suggests that each soul has been divided into a male and female part, so men and women can only be complete when they find their 'soul mate'. Some people believe that this is literally true and that we are all looking for one special person who is our 'other half'. Whether this is right or not, it is certainly true that men and women seek out in their lovers the qualities of the other sex which complement and enhance their own qualities. When a man and woman are right for each other, their loving unites the great polarities of Yin and Yang, and both lovers can experience the Tao. By coming together in love, they find something which is bigger than either of them as individuals, and this can feel as if they have found the other half of their soul. This is because only the right lover can awaken the parts of us that are normally dormant.

The Breath of Life

One of the manifestations of the principles of Yin and Yang is as the in-breath and the out-breath. When practising being aware of your breath (as discussed in Chapter Two), become conscious of your own acceptance and letting go of the air that fills you. The ancient East teaches that breath is more than atoms and molecules: it is also a life-energy which the Chinese call *chi* and the Indians call *prana* – indeed, our word 'spirit' comes from a word meaning breath. Imagine yourself breathing in the very power of life, and, as you exhale, imagine you are releasing all worries, fears and negative energy.

This life-energy is very important in Chinese medicine, such as acupuncture, which teaches that, as well as veins, arteries and a nervous system, we also have a network of energy channels called meridians. These energy channels carry chi around the aura, the energy-body which surrounds the physical body.

Massage relaxes the physical body and invigorates the energy-body. You can enhance this natural process using the power of your mind and massage techniques. A particularly important power-point in the body's energy system is just below the navel. The Chinese call this the *tan tien* and the Indians call it the *hara chakra*. The following massage will help you to invigorate your lover's energy and focus it in the tan tien.

Circulating Energy

This technique will help circulate and balance the subtle energies which surround your lover's body, and centre them in the powerhouse of the tan tien (see page 47). You may wish to repeat the stroke a few times. Kneel alongside your partner's buttocks and, crossing your arms, place a hand on each of your partner's feet (right).
Then, using hardly any pressure, gradually bring your hands up the inside of the legs. As you do so, imagine that you are drawing lines of white light or channels of energy. Ask your lover to help you, by also visualizing this.

Bring your hands over your lover's buttocks (below), and up the outside of the back to the shoulders.

Now stroke down the outside of your lover's arms and from the palms of the hands, lightly return back up the inside of the arms (right), over the shoulders to the top of the spine, visualizing lines of energy as before.

Trail your hands down either
side of your lover's spine (left),
over the buttocks and down the
outside of the legs, completing
the circle at the feet. Then make
clockwise circles with your hand
on the small of your lover's back
(right) to stimulate the tan tien.

Sensual Slide

If you are in an adventurous mood, then play with full body massage. This is an extremely arousing sensual art, highly developed in the East, especially Thailand. For these massage techniques, you will need to cover the whole of the front of your body with a lot of oil, so that you can slide effortlessly across your lover. It may get a little messy – but it will be worth it!

Kneel at your lover's feet and place your breasts against the soles. Taking some of your weight on your arms, slowly slide your well oiled body up the legs (above), letting your belly come into contact with feet and lower legs. Keep moving up, over the buttocks and back, until you are almost lying on top of your lover (right). Then squirm gently in the oily contact between your bodies.

Skin-to-skin Massage

As in full body massage, these techniques are about achieving as much skin-to-skin contact as possible, though they are not so energetic, and are easier to practise. Instead of using the whole body to give the massage, slowly pass the full expanse of your well oiled chest and belly over, firstly, your lover's back, and then the rest of the body (right). Vary the pressure to your partner's preference.

You can also do this with well oiled arms (above). Use the full expanse of both arms and hands, so that as much of your flesh as possible is touching your lover.

'When my beloved returns to the house, I shall make my body into a temple of gladness. Offering this body as an altar of joy, my hair let down will sweep it clean. Then my beloved will consecrate this temple.'

Traditional song

Connecting

Having completed massaging your lover's back, it is time to bring yourselves into harmony again, before asking your partner to turn over. If you have just given a full body massage (page 50), you may like to lie close together, bodies overlapping as much as possible, without the weight becoming unpleasantly heavy (right).

You may prefer to place your head on the pillow of your partner's buttocks (above), or, perhaps, hug him or her lovingly around the waist or legs.

Or kneel, alert and upright, the palms of your hands placed flat on the small of your lover's back.

Close your eyes, be still and at peace. Become aware of your breathing and let it synchronize gradually with your lover's breathing rhythm, so that you are inhaling and exhaling together. Sense the differences in your partner's energy since you have been showering him or her with your loving attentions.

CHAPTER FIVE

Fire and Water

Then she undressed until she was quite naked.
Bahoul fell into an ecstasy
on seeing the beauty and perfection of her form.

He looked at her magnificent thighs
and rebounding navel,
at her belly vaulted like an arch,
her plump breasts standing out like hyacinths.
Her neck was like a gazelle's.
The opening of her mouth was like a ring.
Her lips fresh and red like a gory sabre.
Her teeth might have been taken for pearls,
and her cheeks for roses.
Her eyes were black and well slit.
Her forehead was like the full moon in the night.

Bahoul began to embrace her and suck her lips;
to kiss her bosom and bite her thighs.
So he went on until she was ready to swoon
and could scarcely stammer
and her eyes became veiled.

He looked lovingly on her secret parts,
beautiful enough to attract all eyes
with their purple centre.

Shaykh Nefzawi,
The Perfumed Garden

Man and Woman

In Chinese thought, a man embodies the creative initiating force of Yang and a woman embodies the receptive nurturing power of Yin. This is a sweeping generalization, of course, as everyone contains both Yin and Yang qualities (see Chapter Four), and each individual is completely unique. However, as an underlying principle the idea can help in understanding the complementary natures of man and woman. For instance, in love-making the man embodies the hard and penetrative Yang qualities, while the woman is soft, moist and accommodating – Yin qualities. She receives his semen, which has the creative potential to make her conceive, after which she will nurture and give birth to a new life.

Viewing women as embodiments of Yin qualities doesn't mean that they are seen negatively as totally passive, weak and vulnerable. On the contrary, in Taoism it is the power of Yin which is emphasised and highly praised. In fact, men are encouraged to develop their Yin qualities, to balance out their Yang nature. Giving and receiving sensual massage is seen as an excellent way for a man to develop his softer, more nurturing side.

In the modern West, both men and women have become increasingly dominated by the 'go for it', success-orientated power of Yang. This in itself is fine, but it has become seriously out of balance with the caring, appreciative qualities of Yin. The results are all around us. Enjoying gentle love-play with your partner is a way of enhancing the Yin qualities of just being and enjoying, and letting go, for a while, of the Yang obsession with doing and achieving.

Fire and Water

Taoism is sometimes called the 'way of water'. It delights in apparent paradoxes. In one of its most important books, the *Tao Te Ching*, the Taoist sage, Lao Tsu, says: 'Nothing wears away hard strong rocks, as well as soft weak water. From this, anyone can see that softness is harder than hardness, and weakness is stronger than strength. But no one lives accordingly.' Sensual massage is about using this watery Yin power of softness to overcome the hard resistance of tension and stress. Being made to feel safe and loved, will make your partner able to relax and enjoy.

In Tantra, men are often compared to fire, and women to water. In the conception process, a man's role is brief and dramatic, like fire. A woman nurtures a growing embryo inside her, over time, before giving birth; like water which starts as a spring, becomes a river and eventually reaches the sea. The male is life creating, like the fiery sun. The female is life sustaining, like the rain which makes the fields fertile.

Male sexuality can ignite instantly like fire, burn brightly and be extinguished quickly. Female sexuality often boils slowly, like water, and takes time to cool down. Sensuality and sexuality could be seen like Yin and Yang, as water and fire. Both are, of course, natural and have their unique pleasures. The problem with fire is that it can easily burn out of control. Sensual massage contains the fiery sexual energy, so that it burns more slowly. It allows a woman to come to the boil. Paying attention to after-play as well as foreplay, allows her to cool down while still being loved and nurtured. Like all Taoist and Tantric practices it brings these two qualities into a balanced harmony and wholeness.

A Simple Ritual

You may like to acknowledge these two principles, and the importance of balance between them, by bringing fire and water into the pleasure chamber; perhaps a small bowl of water and a candle, or burning incense stick. You could honour these qualities in each other by performing a simple 'ritual'.

Ask your lover to turn over slowly onto his or her back, and find a relaxed and comfortable position. Once her partner is settled, a woman may gently splash a little water onto her lover's face and body. A man may pass a burning incense stick around his lover. Such rituals often seem foreign to us, but they are encouraged by Taoist and Tantric traditions, in which they are seen as a form of purification, making lovers aware that they are not only loving each other as man and woman, but that they are also embodying the fundamental principles of life.

Rituals are symbolic actions. We all perform rituals everyday, they are not strange or 'religious'. When we shake someone's hand we are engaged in a greeting ritual. Such actions are ways of communicating with our bodies, without using words. The little ritual described here is an opportunity to tell your lover, 'I see in you the great power of femininity or masculinity'.

Playful Touching

Awaken the front of your lover's body to touch, just as you did with the back. Sensually stroke and lightly 'feather' it, scratching, licking and kissing from top to toe. To add to the eroticism, tie a blindfold around your partner's head, as this may make it easier to let go passively into the caresses, and can give an exquisitely sensual feeling of vulnerability (right).

Stroking your lover smoothly with soft velvet (above) can also be erotically stimulating.

'The lover, by applying the nails with love and affection, can bring great comfort to the woman. In fact, there is nothing, perhaps, more delightful to both husband and wife than the skilful use of nails.'

Ananga Ranga

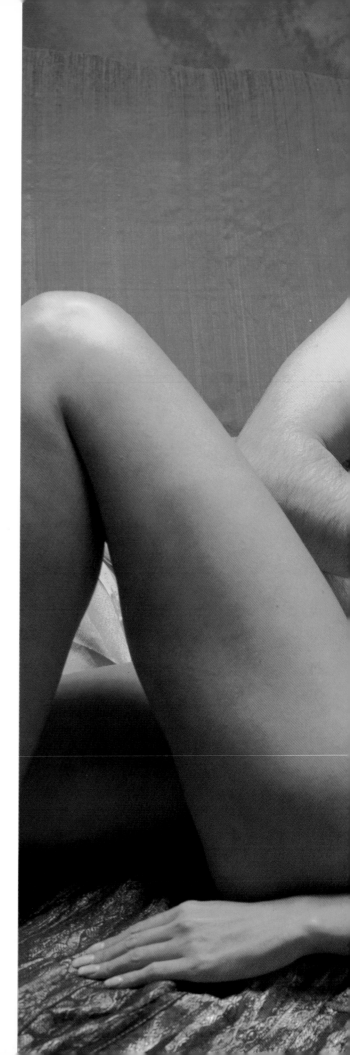

'Feathering'

The touch of a feather is very sensual. Try using a real feather (choose a large, soft, clean one), or a long feather boa. Slowly, glide the feather across your lover's body (left). Try alternating between scratching lightly with the spine, and stroking with the edges. The inside of the elbow is an especially sensitive place to delight in this way.

Pass the feather through your lover's toes (above), and across the palms of the hands.

Scenting the feather with some perfume or aftershave, and passing it under your lover's nose, will give a beautiful aromatic experience (above).

In some ancient traditions using a bird's feather is thought to evoke its spirit, which will come down and give blessings. The eagle is regarded as a divine bird because it flies so high and can see so clearly; so, an eagle feather is said to be particularly auspicious.

Heat Sensations

In Tantra, a man is likened to fire, and a woman is likened to water. Playing with contrasting sensations of hot and cold echoes this polarity and can generate wonderful sensations.

First, place a pleasantly hot face cloth or damp sponge on your lover's belly (above), then follow this with an ice cube (right). Move the ice cube slowly around. Now return to the warm face cloth or sponge. Interchange the two sensations on your lover's body, anywhere that he or she finds pleasant. This can be as enjoyable to the sense of touch as sweet-and-sour food is to your palate!

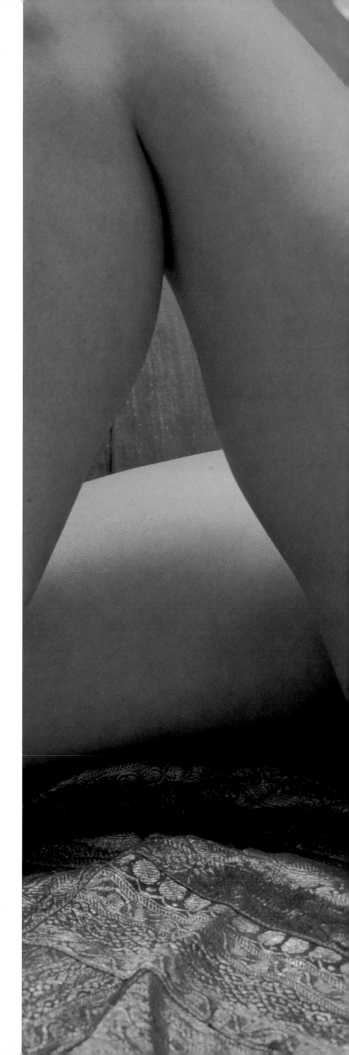

Letting go of the Legs

Ask your partner to relax completely. Taking all of the weight, lift up one of the relaxed legs, one hand supporting it at the calf, the other at the thigh (left). Slowly, bend the leg at the knee, and circle the whole leg to open up the thigh joint. If your lover has really let go, the leg will feel like a dead weight. Although relaxing totally sounds easy, people often find it difficult. Be patient, encouraging your partner to surrender the leg completely, as you move it gently in space. This is also a powerful technique for developing trust.

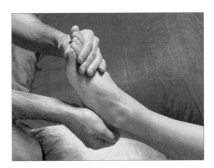

Hold your lover's foot in two hands, with one hand at the top and the other on the heel. Lift the foot slightly and gently rock it to and fro (above). Then make circles in space with the toes, exploring the gentle movement of the ankle joint. When ready, move on to your lover's other leg and foot.

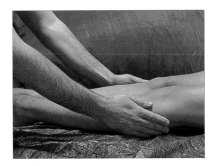

You will need massage oil again from now on. Place your palms on the outside of your lover's shins (above), then sweep your hands up the outside of the legs, across the tops of the thighs, down the inside of the legs, and back to the feet. Repeat this movement a few times.

Letting go of the Arms

Kneel alongside your lover's arms. Pick up the arm nearest to you, holding the top with one hand, and the forearm with the other (right). Encourage your partner to let go completely, so that the arm feels like a heavy dead weight in your hands. Move the arm gently in space, allowing it to ease open the shoulder joint and the elbow. This can be a surprisingly sensual experience.

Circle the top of your lover's arm with both hands, so that your thumbs and fingers meet, and your palms are touching the arm (right).

With gentle pressure, slide your hands down your lover's arm until you reach the wrist, pulling the arm slightly as you go (right).

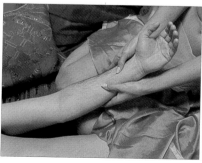

The inside of the elbow is extremely sensitive. Take a few moments to stroke your lover softly there, with your fingertips (right). Then continue with the hand massages on the following pages, before moving on to the other arm and hand.

Pleasuring the Hands

Take your lover's hand, palm uppermost, into your hands, as shown in the photograph (right). Use your thumbs to knead the palm gently, and your fingers to massage the back of the hand. Starting in the sensitive centre, work out slowly to the knuckles.

Use your fingers and thumb to knead gently your lover's finger joints. Start near to the palms and work out slowly to the fingertips (left).

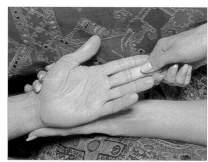

With a light, sensual touch, stroke your lover's palm with your fingers. Take each of your lover's fingers in turn and pull them gently away from the hand, letting the finger slip slowly out of your grasp (left).

Lightly pass your tongue over the sensitive inside of your lover's palm, pausing to blow gently with your warm breath (left). Explore the soft skin between the fingers. When ready, move to your lover's other arm and hand.

CHAPTER SIX

The Power of the Mind

She came out
like the rising dawn
after an obscure night,
or the water of immortality
gushing
from a dark cavern.

She carried in her hands
a bowl of snow-water
into which sugar had been poured,
and essences of roses mixed.

I knew not
whether she had perfumed it with rose-water,
or whether a few drops from her rosy face
had fallen into it.

I took the beverage
from her beautiful hands,
drank it,
and began to live again.

Sa'di,
The Rose Garden

The Imagination

In the modern West we have a very limited view of the imagination, seeing it as unreal, and often irrelevant to our everyday lives: we say 'That's just your imagination'. The Tantric tradition, however, sees the imagination as a powerful faculty, the seed-bed of creation. Everything that is created exists first as an idea in someone's imagination.

Consciousness is seen as a clear light, with the imagination as a film held before it. The Tantric master, Aryadeva, said: 'Just as a clear gem is coloured by other objects around it, so also is the gem of the mind coloured by the constructive imagination.'

The ancient East developed many mental practices which use the power of the imagination for healing, pleasure and experiencing mystical states of awareness. In Taoism and Tantra, the mind is not seen as separate from the body, but closely connected. When the body is ill, we feel bad. When the mind is troubled, we often become ill. The Chinese sometimes talk of the 'body-mind' as one thing. Changing the state of the body can change the state of the mind, and changing the state of the mind can change the body. Physical massage calms the mind, and mental visualization relaxes the body.

Visualization

Before beginning the head massages in this chapter, try guiding your lover in a visualization, which can help in finding a deep state of relaxation. Kneel behind your partner's head, and hold it gently, with one of your palms covering the forehead and the other under the back of the head at the base of the skull. Ask your partner to close his or her eyes. This position is very emotionally calming.

Ask your lover to bring to mind a favourite place, where he or she feels especially happy and at ease. You could suggest an imaginary place, such as a tropical island, lush forest, calm sea, mountain peak. Encourage your lover to imagine being there, by asking him or her to describe sensations and feelings. If this is difficult, ask questions: 'What is it you like about this place?', 'What can you see?', 'What can you hear?', or 'What can you smell?'. Suggest an imaginary exploration of this special place, to find somewhere comfortable to lie down and soak in the peaceful ambience.

This use of the imagination is not designed to stop your lover from being present in the moment with you. Rather, it is more as if you are being taken on a little journey into his or her imaginary world.

Lovers of God

The fifteenth-century Indian mystic poet Kabir used the imagination to see his soul as God's lover. He writes about longing for God like one pining for an absent beloved:

When I am separated from my Beloved, my
heart weeps;
My days are without comfort and my nights
without sleep.
Who can understand my sadness?
The night is so dark, and the hours slip by.
Because my love is away,
I start up – trembling all over with fear.

Kabir was born a Muslim, but studied under a Hindu guru, so is respected by both religions. The Islamic mystics are called Sufis and they too often wrote about God as if talking about a physical lover. Ayn Hamadani was an eleventh-century Sufi poet who wrote in extremely erotic terms about this divine affair. He so outraged the religious authorities that he was executed. His poems contain wonderful sensual imagery:

She embraced me in the night.
My idol entwined me in her arms.
She captured me and pierced me
With a ring that showed I was her slave.
I exclaimed, 'For this loving I'll cry, I'll rage,
I'll frenzy...'
But she closed my mouth with her sweet lips.

Just as these mystic poets used their creative imaginations to see themselves as God's intimate lovers, so you may like to see your lover as an embodiment of this higher power. All the spiritual traditions of the world tell us that each of us is a spark of the 'One Light'. As you caress each other, imagine that you are sharing a divine love affair with the higher power that created and sustains you both; through loving each other, you are loving love itself.

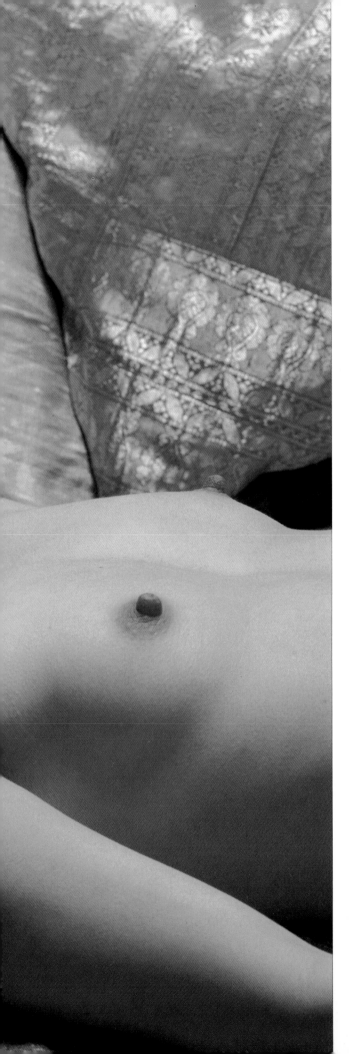

Soothing the Scalp

You will not need massage oil for these techniques. Kneel behind your lover's head, supporting it with both hands. Lift it slightly, taking all the weight of the head (left). Pull it gently away from the neck, then tilt it to the left and right, releasing the muscles in the neck.

The scalp is deliciously sensual. Place your fingers and thumbs on your lover's head. Starting with both thumbs together at the crown, push in and then let go (above). Slowly, knead all of the scalp with thumbs and fingers, making little circular movements, applying pressure and then releasing.

Comb your fingers through your lover's hair. Start close to the scalp. As you move the fingers slowly away from the head, occasionally close them, so that hair is trapped between them and pulled slightly. Then release the hair and let it flow freely again (above).

Releasing Tension

Place the fingertips of both hands on your lover's temples, with the thumbs flat over the middle of the forehead (right). Gently rotate your fingers, massaging the temples. Then, softly, sweep your thumbs across the brow, towards your fingers.

Place your fingertips at the jaw joint, just in front of your lover's ears, under the cheekbones (above). Most people hold a lot of tension here. Release these muscles with little circular movements, applying pressure and then releasing.

Stroke up your lover's neck and chin with the flat of your fingers (above). Use light flicking movements, as if brushing crumbs off a table.

Relaxing the Eyes

Using your thumbs, or two fingers, apply gentle pressure to the ridge of bone which forms the top of your lover's eye sockets (left). Starting near the nose, move slowly along the eye sockets, pressing and releasing.

Repeat on the lower edge of your lover's eye sockets (above).

Gently place one thumb onto each of your lover's closed eyes, near the nose. Very lightly, slide the thumb across the eyeball to the other side of the eye (above).

Mouth Music

Place one finger from each hand under your lover's lower lip, so that the fingertips touch in the middle (left). Slowly move the fingers apart, applying pressure then releasing. Trace the contours of the bottom of the mouth in this way...

...and then repeat on the top lip.

Place your two fingers on the cheek bone, either side of your lover's nose (above). Follow the shape of the cheek bone to the edge of the face – applying pressure and releasing.

Stroking the Ears

Having your ears massaged softly can be extremely pleasant, as there is an energy channel which links them to the sexual areas of the body. Gently, roll the edges of your lover's ear between your thumb and forefinger. Start at the top near the head, and move slowly around the edge of the ear (right). When you reach the fleshy lobe, pull it gently, letting finger and thumb slide across it, so that they eventually slip off the ear altogether. You can massage both ears at once, but it may be easier to tilt your lover's head to one side and do one ear at a time.

Place your finger behind your lover's ear lobe (above), and sensually move your whole finger up behind the ear.

Completely cover both of your lover's ears with the palms of your hands, and rest them there for a while (above), so that your lover can enjoy the sound of silence.

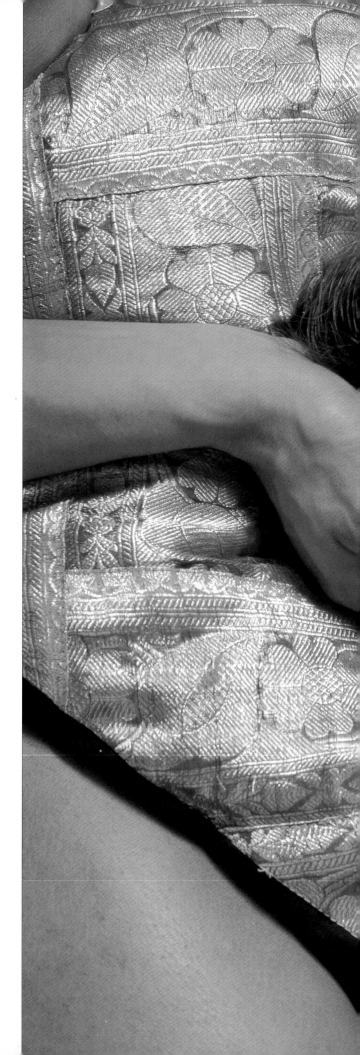

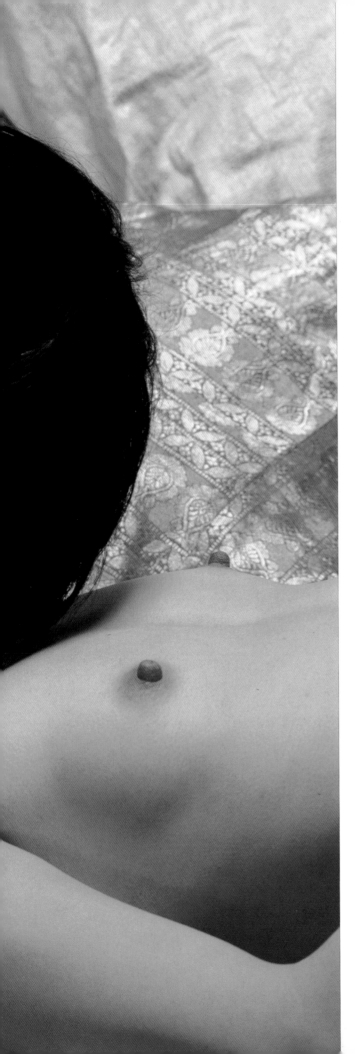

Delighting the Face

*Keeping your lover's ears covered, reach across
and kiss him or her on the lips (left). Try holding
one lip between your two lips, pulling it slightly
until it slips out of your mouth. Because the ears
are covered, your lover will have the unusual
sensation of hearing as well as feeling your kiss.*

*Release your hands, and explore your lover's ear
with your tongue (above). This can send ripples of
pleasure through the whole body.*

*Cover the eyes, and gently kiss your lover
on the lips (above).*

'When a woman is excited with passion,
she should cover her lover's eyes with her
hands and, closing her own eyes, thrust
her tongue into his mouth. She should
move it to and fro, and in and out, with
a pleasant motion suggestive of more
intimate forms of enjoyment to come.'

Ananga Ranga

CHAPTER SEVEN

The Erotic Imagination

Visualise yourself as an erotic red goddess:
Symbol of dedication and passion.

Three eyes – blazing with passion:
Her tongue is lustful,
with the purifying power of her inner fire.

She is naked, with dishevelled hair:
Symbolic of freedom
from the bonds of delusion.

She is the intuition:
A reminder that everything must pass.

Blazing like a fire:
She expresses her wisdom-essence,
by embracing her lover without restraint.

Chakrasambhara Tantra

Tantra

Tantra began about 5,000 BC in India, as a cult of the Hindu god Siva and his consort Sakti. According to Tantric tradition, they made love, and, as a result, Sakti gave form to Siva's spirit, and the universe was created. In Tantra, therefore, all that exists finds its foundation in this primal sexual act. Tantra flourished as a non-conformist and rebellious alternative to the orthodox teachings of the Hindu brahmin priesthood.

Many conventional Hindus held that celibacy and asceticism were prerequisites for experiencing enlightenment. For practitioners of Tantra, periods of celibacy were seen as spiritually healthy, just as occasional fasting is physically healthy. They also saw abstinence as a way of channelling sexual energy in other directions. The idea that celibacy was essential to a spiritual life, however, was seen as ridiculous. How could natural human sexuality preclude knowledge of God?

The word Tantra means weaving, appropriately, as Tantric philosophy brings together many, often paradoxical, aspects of life and spins them into one thread. Where other philosophies see a contradiction, Tantra sees a creative dynamic tension. Sexuality is not thought to oppose spirituality. It is an opportunity to partake in the divine union of Siva and Sakti. Tantra makes sex a sacred art. In the ancient Indian language, Sanskrit, the root of the word for art means 'appropriately united'. Tantra is the art of union.

Tantra also means 'expansion', and Tantric practitioners use life's varied experiences, including sensuality, to expand their own awareness, to help them become fully conscious of all that they are. The psychologist, C. G. Jung said that 'sexuality is the spokesperson for the instincts'. Tantra embraces these basic sexual instincts, and, by so doing, transforms them into spiritual ecstasy.

The Deeper Experience

Tantra has had a profound influence on Buddhist as well as Hindu traditions. Many of its practices are complex and require great spiritual discipline: the contents of this book are only a small part of a great mountain of wisdom. In India, spiritual practice is called 'yoga', a Sanskrit word meaning union. Tantra is a sexual yoga, a way of coming into union with God using the natural pleasures of sensuality. There are many Hindu temples covered with statues and pictures of couples performing every type of sexual act. This is not some sort of primitive pornography, but a reflection of the idea of sexual love as a type of worship.

Some Tantric practices involve lovers visualizing themselves as particular gods and goddesses while making love, as in the extract from the *Chakrasambhara Tantra* which opens this chapter. Such ideas sound exotic and peculiar to most westerners, largely because we do not fully understand them. We are used to one divine God, so, imagining ourselves as God seems absurd or blasphemous. Hindus and Buddhists also believe in one ultimate unity, but for them, the different aspects of this divine oneness are embodied by various gods and goddesses. The qualities of these mythic personalities are all within human beings. By associating with them in our imagination, we find these qualities in ourselves.

Although specific Tantric practices like these may be culturally alien to modern westerners, the essence of Tantric wisdom remains relevant. Life is a spiritual journey towards a deeper experience of what it is to be human; and all of life is a part of that journey. Sexuality, in particular, gives an opportunity to discover the divine spark within. Life is a sexual dance of the great primal forces; spirit and matter, Siva and Sakti.

The Erotic Imagination

Although complex erotic visualizations are unnecessarily technical for most of us, we can still use the power of the imagination to enhance our love-play. We do this quite naturally, and often privately, in our sexual fantasies, which we usually feel embarrassed to share, even with a trusted lover. In Tantra, however, nothing is taboo. If you feel something, it is better to acknowledge it than to push it away. Most sexual fantasies are a harmless and enjoyable means of increasing arousal.

Try using sensual massage as an opportunity to share these erotic imaginings. During this intimate time together, lovers feel safe and accepted, and more able to open up the private world of the imagination. While massaging, ask your lover to share with you a favourite, very arousing fantasy. If this is difficult, you can help by asking questions: 'Is there somewhere you would particularly like to make love?', 'Is there a way of making love that you would like to try?', or, 'Is there something I could say or do that would really excite you?'

You may like to share your own fantasies while you are massaging your lover, who would then be the recipient of your erotic imagination as well as your touch. Remember these fantasies: you and your lover might consider acting them out at some other time.

Circles on Soft Skin

Make your lover's belly sensitive and ready for your touch, by giving it little kisses, and blowing gently (left).

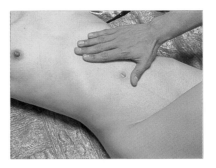

You will need massage oil again from now on. Place the palm of one hand lightly on your lover's belly. Make slow circles with your hand (above), starting at the edge of the belly and working gradually in towards the navel.

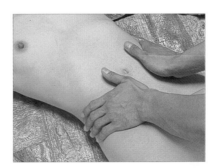

Place your palms on the sides of your lover's belly, fingers towards the small of the back. With gentle pressure, move your hands slowly towards your lover's navel, pulling the soft skin a little on the way (above).

Caressing the Breasts

The breasts are a highly erogenous zone. Take your lover's breasts in both hands (right), and gently knead them, applying pressure and then releasing. Start at the edge of the breast and gradually move in towards the nipple. Divide your attention between both breasts, or, concentrate first on one and then on the other. If massaging a man, run your hands lightly over his chest.

The nipples are very sensitive, for men and women. Circle your lover's nipple softly, using one finger (above). Some people enjoy their nipples being tweaked gently between finger and thumb. This may cause the nipple to go hard and erect.

Circle your lover's nipple lightly with your tongue (above), and then blow softly on it with your warm breath.

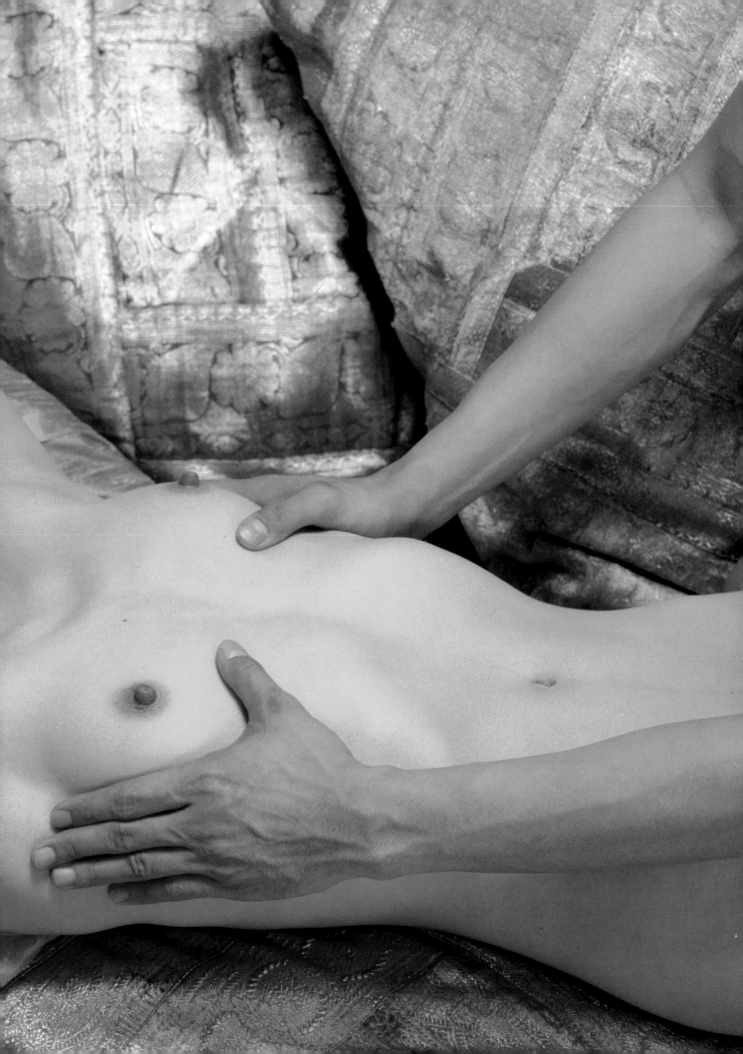

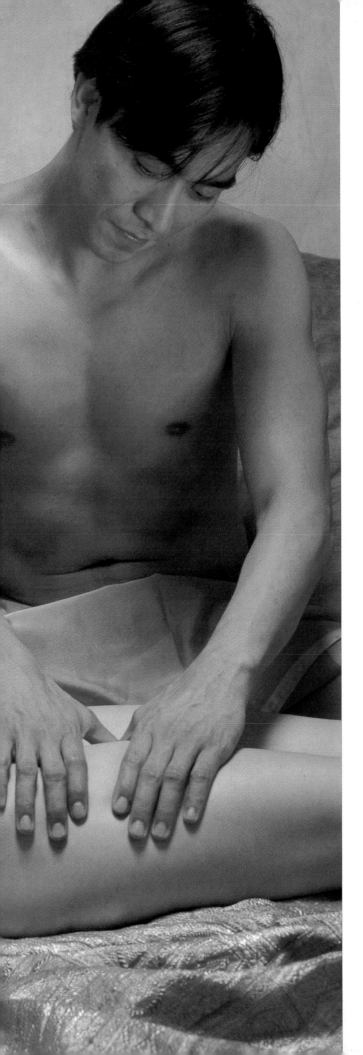

Massaging the Thighs

Kneel by your lover's legs and place both palms on one of his or her thighs. Starting near the knee, gently knead the soft flesh, moving gradually up the thigh to the top of the leg (left). As you massage the inner thigh, let your arm brush provocatively across your lover's genitals, teasing them by hinting at what is to come.

Place your palms flat on your lover's inner thigh, fingers pointing down (above). Applying gentle pressure, pull the hands up, slightly stretching the soft skin. Starting near the knee, work gradually up to the top of the thigh, before moving on to massage the other leg.

'Women are peonies, spring flowers, lotuses and bowers.
Women are pomegranates, peaches, melons and pearls.
Women are receptacles, crucibles, vessels and worlds.
Women are the fruit of life, the nourishing force of nature.'

Tao Tsung-I

Harmonizing the Energy-body

You have now massaged the whole of your lover's body, and are ready to bring your loving attention to the highly sensitive genital area. Before doing this, circulate the energy as you did for the back of the body. You won't need massage oil. Use two fingers from each hand.

Place two fingers on each of your partner's feet and, using hardly any pressure, gradually bring your fingers up the inside of both legs (below). As you do so, imagine you are drawing lines of white light, or channels of energy. Ask your lover to help, by also visualizing this.

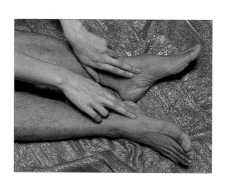

Using hardly any pressure, bring your fingers over the top of your lover's thighs, then up the outside of the belly and chest (right), and down the outside of the arms. From the palms of your lover's hands, trail your fingers lightly up the

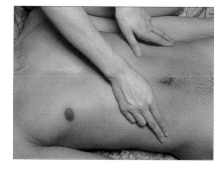

inside of the arms (right), over the shoulders to the top of the breast bone. Trail your fingers down the centre of the chest, over the outside of the thighs, and down the outside of the legs, completing a circle at the feet. Repeat this a few times.

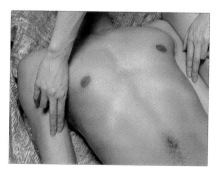

The energy centre of the heart chakra can be stimulated by making small, light, clock-wise circles, with the fingertips of one hand, on the centre of your lover's chest (above). Imagine the heart is opening, like a flower coming into bloom.

CHAPTER EIGHT

Riding the Crest of a Wave

The lovers took off their clothes,
and sat side by side within the silken net,
on coverlets of the rarest silk,
perfumed with orchids and musk.

They laughed and played together,
until the flush of desire mounted to their brow,
and the passion in their hearts made them tremble.

They then performed the mystery of the clouds and rain,
and whatever the wine inspired.
He sat on the bed,
and the lady of the vase played the flute for him:

Not from bamboo or stone, not played on strings,
this is the song of an instrument that lives,
that makes the emerald tassels quiver.

Who can say what the tune is, or the key?
The red lips open wide.
The slender fingers play their part daintily.
Deep in – deep out.
Their hearts grow wild with passion.
There are no words to tell of the ecstasy that thrills.

The Golden Lotus

The Gateway to Life and the Weapon of Love

In the passage from the Chinese classic *The Golden Lotus*, which opens this chapter, playing the flute is a euphemism for fellatio (oral sex performed on a man). The writings of the ancient East are full of such delightfully colourful names and phrases. They have an air of romance and mysticism in contrast to our often clinical or crude western terminology.

One of the names for cunnilingus (oral sex performed on a woman), is 'drinking from the spring of immortality'. The vagina is called 'secret garden', 'pleasure garden', 'gateway to life', 'honey pot', 'shady valley of joy', 'jade garden', 'open melon' and 'secret crevice'. As well as being likened to a flute, the penis is called 'jade stalk', 'mountain crag', 'weapon of love', 'henchman', 'warrior' and, echoing western imagery, 'cockerel'. In India, it is known as the 'Siva lingam' (Siva's penis), the embodiment of the cosmic creativity of the god Siva. The yoni (vagina), is the entrance to the sacred shrine, the ultimate symbol of receptivity.

Thus, in the ancient East, the genitals were not treated as vulgar, or somehow separate from the rest of the body. They were honoured and respected, as the supreme embodiments of the gods and goddesses of Tantra, and the Yin and Yang principles of Taoism. In the West, we tend to treat the genitals as completely different from the other parts of the body. They are often seen as unclean, and are kept hidden. We don't often think of massaging them. This was certainly not the attitude of the ancient East, where the practice of massaging these areas, with hands and mouth, was developed as a fine art. Rather than orgasm, the aim was to build sexual desire to a peak, by taking one's lover to the brink of orgasm, only to pull him or her back. In this way, the whole body, not just the sexual organs, can become involved in the experience. You can help your lover to 'ride the crest of the wave' of ecstasy, like a surfer. It is the pleasure of the ride, not the destination, which is important. There is immense erotic enjoyment in being made to wait for what you want!

In the modern West, oral eroticism is seen more and more as an intimate and natural part of loving foreplay, though, up until quite recently, it was seen as perverse. The Tantric and Taoist view is that it is both a highly enjoyable and deeply spiritual act. There is a major energy channel which connects the top lip of the mouth to the genitals, which is one reason why kissing is so erotic. Placing the mouth on the genitals means that the upper energies of one lover can circulate naturally with the lower energies of the other lover, which is stimulating for both.

Orgasm

Some schools of thought in the East encourage a man not to ejaculate, or to do so only infrequently. They believe that semen is a valuable life-essence which should be conserved, and they teach techniques for achieving orgasm without ejaculation. This means that a man can continue to make love after orgasm, and more fully satisfy his woman. For most of us, this is too technical and inhibits the natural flow. The important point is that ejaculation is not the goal. Tantra and Taoism encourage holding back simply because it heightens the sexual energy, not from any sense of moral obligation.

Orgasm is a great release of energy, and an opportunity to reach spiritual heights together. You may want to use the following oral and manual massages of the genitals to take your lover to orgasm, or as a preliminary to full sexual intercourse. Some people, particularly women, are capable of multiple orgasm, and so could do both. Other people, also mainly women, find achieving orgasm very difficult or impossible. Sensual massage can help because it is relaxing and thoroughly stimulating. The important thing is to enjoy your love-making, anyway.

The art of Taoist and Tantric foreplay raises the sexual energy to fever pitch, by stimulating the whole body and the mind. You have been on a sensual journey towards the following, highly erotic massages of the yoni and the lingam. Now that you are here, take the time to really enjoy them. If you feel that your lover is approaching orgasm, pause for a while and pleasure another part of the body. Lead your lover continually to the edge, before finally letting him or her fly over. Each peak of pleasure may be followed by a trough, but the next peak will be higher, and the next higher still.

The joy of massage is that your lover is completely passive, so can be tantalized and teased. If you are being massaged, try not to hurry things. Just lie back and let go. Enter the ebb and flow of the waves of pleasure that your lover's attentions are creating.

You may want to hold back from orgasm, but find this difficult. It can be helpful and enjoyable to return attention to the breath (as discussed in Chapter Two). Enjoy the sensations of pleasure and arousal, rising and falling, within an overall awareness of the breath flowing in and out. Putting some space around the sensations in this way is an important Tantric technique. It can inhibit unwanted ejaculation, and can also take the whole experience to new spiritual depths.

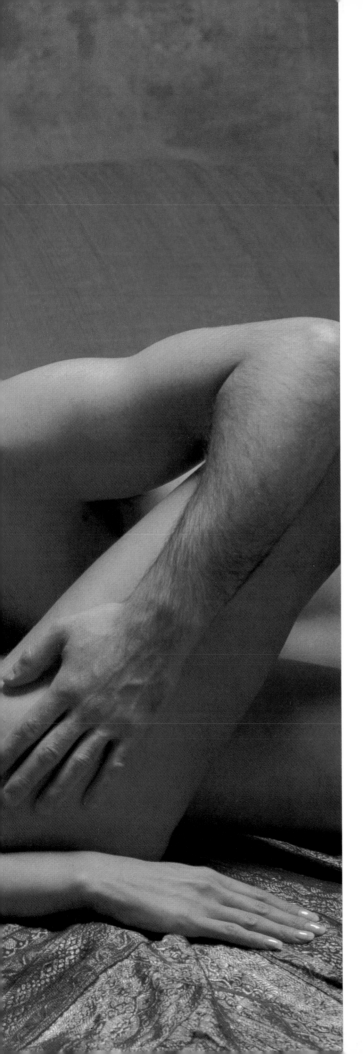

The Blissful Temple of the Body

The ancients honoured the body as a temple of the soul. In the Tantric tradition, lovers touched each other with reverence and sacred respect. Place your head lightly on your lover's stomach as if you were lying on a temple altar. Feel the rise and fall of his or her breath. Slowly and provocatively, stroke the inside of the thighs. Tease your lover by occasionally brushing your hand across the secret garden or jade stalk.

'Here in this body are the sacred rivers, here are the sun and moon, as well as the pilgrimage places. I have not encountered another temple as blissful as my own body.'

Saraha Doha

105

Exploring the Pleasure Garden

Place one palm flat over your lover's yoni. Stroke it upwards over the pubic bone. Immediately, follow with your other hand. Alternate the hands slowly and smoothly. Tenderly explore her secret garden with your fingers. Women respond in different ways, and can respond differently at different times. Listen to your lover's body language. Try softly massaging the vulva lips.

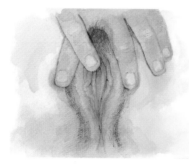

Holding the lips open, stroke the protruding clitoris gently (above). This is especially stimulating. Make sure your finger is moist. Try circling around the clitoris and rubbing softly.

Place one palm across your lover's lower belly. Slowly insert the index and middle fingers from your other hand into her pleasure garden (above). The fingers should be slightly bent, pads upwards. When inside, move your fingers as if beckoning someone. This will stimulate the pleasurable spot, sometimes called the G-spot, inside the yoni. Let your lover guide you to the right place. Try massaging one of her breasts at the same time.

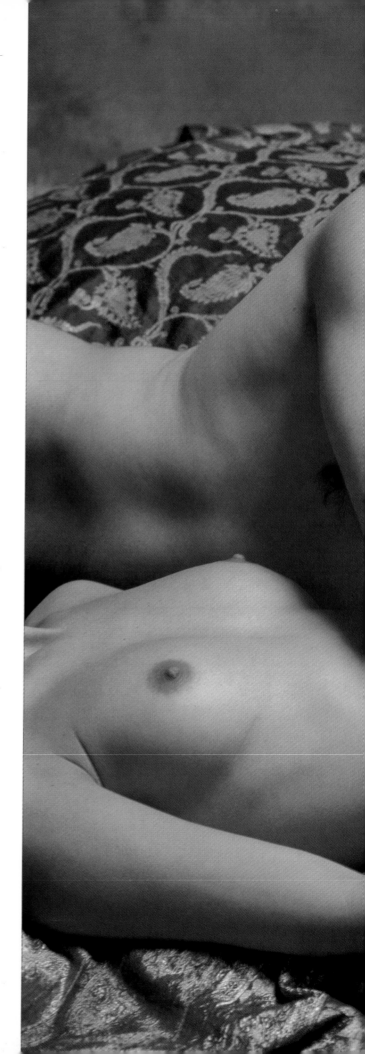

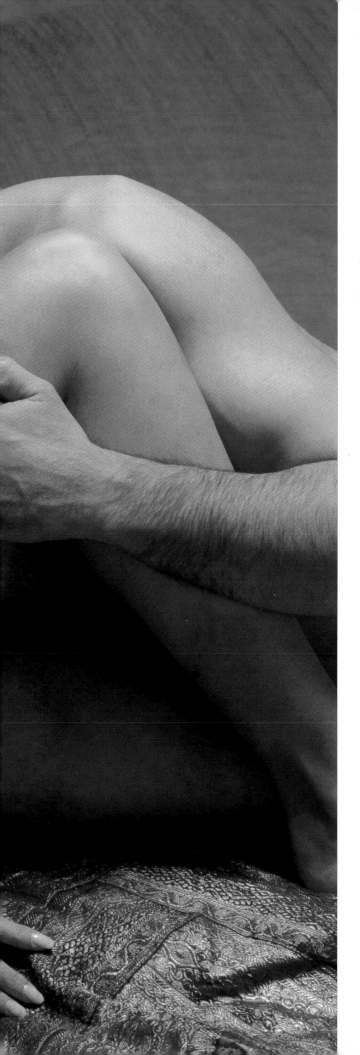

Drinking from the Spring of Immortality

Cover your lover's thighs with little kisses (left), pausing occasionally to blow softly with warm breath, or teasingly kiss and blow around her yoni, and then return to the thighs. In The Perfumed Garden, Shaykh Nefzawi says: 'The yoni like the mouth has two lips and a tongue.' Kiss your lover's secret garden as you would her mouth; delicately passing over her lips with yours, passionately exploring with your tongue deep within her, and playing softly with her clitoris, as you would her tongue. Kiss the lips of your lover's vulva and explore her spring of immortality with long soft movements of your tongue.

Stimulate your lover's sensitive clitoris with your tongue (above). Begin by circling it slowly. Then let your tongue pass over it with a soft luxurious motion. Also try extremely light and quick darting movements. Let your protruding tongue enter your lover's secret pleasure garden. Move it in and out, circling to explore all the inner edges of her yoni.

Pleasuring the Jade Stalk

Place one palm over your lover's scrotum. Stroke gently upwards over his jade stalk and pubic bone, to the belly. Follow immediately with your other hand. Alternate the hands, with a slow smooth rhythm. Whether his lingam is erect or flaccid, you can pleasure him with these massages.

Play tenderly with his jade stalk. Men respond in different ways, and can respond differently at different times. Listen to your lover's body language. Try wrapping one well oiled hand around the base of his lingam, with your thumb at the base (above). With gentle pressure, pull your hand up and off. Replace it immediately with the other hand, alternating with a smooth rhythm.

The top of your lover's lingam is especially sensitive. Circle this area with a moist finger, paying attention to the soft area on one side. Soft stimulation here can lead to a build up of exquisite pleasure. Wrap one hand around your lover's lingam (above). With a smooth deliberate rhythm, move your hand up and down, pulling the foreskin back a little as you do so, and perhaps playing gently with your lover's scrotum at the same time.

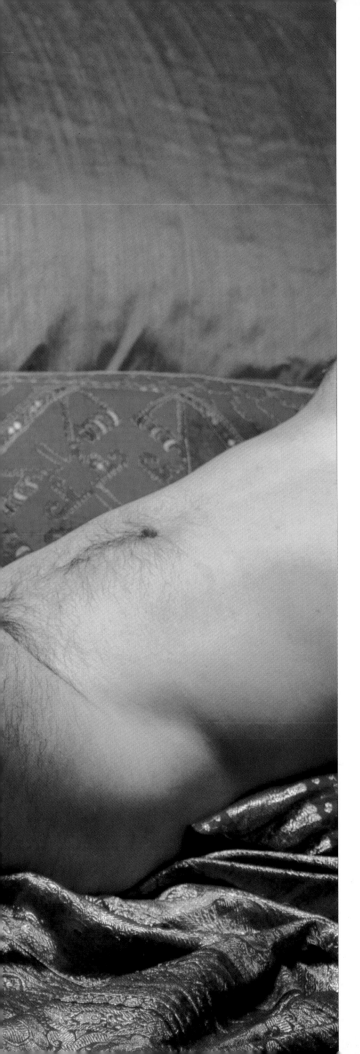

Playing Siva's Flute

Cover your lover's thighs with little kisses, pausing to blow softly with warm breath (left). Tease him by occasionally kissing and blowing around his lingam, and then returning to the thighs. Explore gently with your tongue all around your lover's lingam. The Kama Sutra regards fellatio as great sexual art. It lists eight different variations, with exotic names like 'sucking a mango fruit'.

Cover the shaft of his jade stalk with long luxurious strokes. Delight the tip with extremely light darting movements (above).

If you want to, take the whole of your lover's lingam into your mouth, as deeply as is comfortable (above). Move your mouth back and forth along the shaft, being careful of your teeth. While his jade stalk is in your mouth, play with it gently with your tongue. Some men like the hot and cold sensation of ice in a woman's mouth while the lingam is being sucked. Cold wine, yogurt, soft fruits, and so on, are also found to be pleasurable.

Mutual Pleasuring

*If you wish to mutually pleasure each other,
lie head to toe so that you can delight each other
with your tongues.*

*You can also mutually pleasure each other with
your hands, either both at the same time, or
taking it in turns to give and receive (above).*

*Or, while you are pleasuring your lover's
secret garden or jade stalk with your tongue
or hand, he or she may like to massage your
feet or hands (above).*

CHAPTER NINE

Falling and Flying

At the end of loving,
he should embrace her
and with agreeable words cause her to drink
from a cup held in his own hand,
or he may give her water to drink.

They can then eat sweetmeats,
or anything else according to their liking,
and may drink the juice of mango fruits,
or anything known to be sweet, soft and pure.

The lovers may also sit on the porch
of the palace or house
enjoying the moonlight and conversing happily.
At this time too,
while the woman lies in his lap
with her face towards the moon,
let him show her the different planets,
the morning star, the polar star,
and the seven Rishis or Great Bear.

Kama Sutra

La Petite Mort

The French call orgasm *la petite mort*, the little death, echoing the wisdom of the ancient East, where orgasm can be a mystical release, and, as in death, orgasm gives the opportunity to transcend our normal awareness of ourselves as limited separate beings, and merge for a moment in the oneness of life: flying up to the heights of heaven, and falling back into an ocean of love.

This transcendental sexual experience is beautifully described by author and lover, D. H. Lawrence, in *Women in Love*:

'How can I say I love you, when I have ceased to be. We are both caught up and transcended into a new awareness, where everything is silent because there is nothing to answer. All is perfect and at one. Speech travels between the separate parts, but, in the perfect one, there is the perfect silence of bliss.'

Taoist and Tantric mystics say that this blissful state is a taste of reality that is always present.

Most of the time we don't notice it, because we are so caught up in in thinking about life – worrying about the future and remembering the past. Making love is such a powerful sensual experience that it can help us to let go of our notions about who we think we are, and what we believe life is all about. For a brief, pleasurable moment we are living fully in the present, unconcerned with our usual, day-to-day opinions and preconceptions. Like a little child at play, we are just enjoying what is happening.

Normally, we think of ourselves as people with names and certain characteristics – some of which we like and some which we don't. The mystics teach us that these are not our true identities, but only shells which we inhabit for the short time we call a life. The Taoist sage Lao Tsu says: 'The reason you have troubles is because you think you are your personality. If you saw through this, you'd have no problems.'

Our real souls are eclipsed by the personalities we assume we have, and this cuts us off from the great spirit of love which fills the universe. Most spiritual practices are designed to allow in an intuitive sense of who we really are. In the love and passion of sensuality, our ideas about things cease to be so important, and we can glimpse the still and compassionate nature of the soul.

The Heart of Life

The moment of orgasm may be only brief, but if it is fully entered into, it can be transforming. There is a great release of tension. We emerge softer and deeply contented. You have been 'making' love and now you may bathe in this love you have created together. Treasure this time. Hold your lover close and pamper him or her. Give as much attention to the after-play as you have to the foreplay, with stroking, little kisses, appreciation and synchronized breathing. Merge in the stillness, and dive into the depths of your emotional connection.

Gaze deeply into each other's eyes, without saying anything. If you sense any barriers of embarrassment or fear, just be aware of your breath, and let them go. The eyes are said to be the gateway to the soul. Look beyond your lover's eyes, and into the soul. Look beyond the personality to the indefinable mysterious presence that is looking back at you, experiencing the joys and sorrows of his or her own life, as you do yours. Look beyond even this, until you see in your lover's eyes the oneness of the universe. It is as if you are looking at yourself.

Lovers are two hearts meeting in the one great heart of the omnipresent power of love. It is not only a wonderful emotional experience that you share. It is also a taste of the most fundamental force of life. Perhaps we should not talk of 'falling in love', but rather of 'falling into love', for the love is always there, waiting to catch us whenever we take each other's hands and jump into it.

Let your minds be empty and your hearts be full. Meet each other beyond the dance of changing appearances, in the stillness of eternity. Allow yourselves to dissolve into the ocean of love, so that there is no lover and no beloved — only love itself. Life is so full of confusion and suffering; those beautiful moments when we truly commune with each other are like rare and delicate flowers, to be nurtured, nourished and, above all, appreciated.

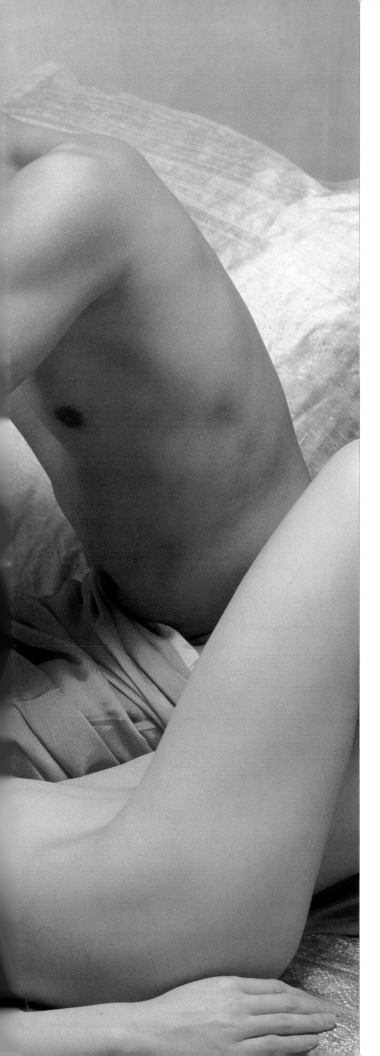

Massaging the Aura

You may like to end your love-play with the most delicate massage of all, massaging your lover's aura, the subtle energy-body that encloses the physical body. For this technique you will not need to touch your partner at all, just hold your hands lightly about 5–10 cm (2–4 in) away from the skin. Pass your hands over your lover's head, using slow, deliberate, sweeping movements.

You may feel a sensation of heat in the palms of your hands. In this very sensitized state, it is also possible that your lover will feel the aura being massaged, even though the skin is not being touched.

Move steadily down the body with expansive circular movements (above), until you reach the feet. When you have finished, flick your hands into space, as if removing droplets of water, as at the beginning of the massage session. This will remove any unwanted energies that may have been picked up from your lover's aura during the massage.

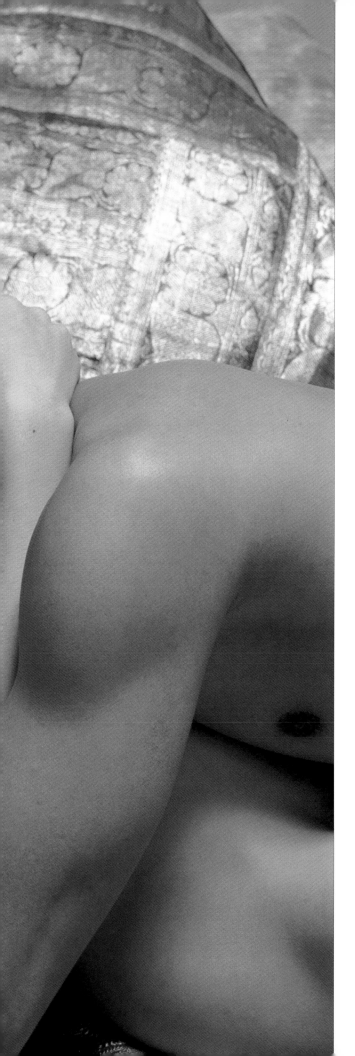

The Shared Heart

Now is the time to bathe in the love you have shared; to hold each other and, maybe, to fall asleep. Find a position that feels intimate and restful, not necessarily a familiar position regularly used for sleeping. You could lie head to toe, embracing each other's legs or face to face (below).

Most often a man holds a woman, but you could try the specially intimate feeling of a woman holding a man (left). Whichever position you choose, in your minds let yourselves merge into one body and your 'shared heart'.

'Life leads the thoughtful person
on a path of many windings.

Now the course is checked,
now it runs straight again.
Here winged thoughts
may pour freely forth in words.
There the heavy burden of knowledge
must be shut away in silence.

But when two people are as one
in their innermost hearts,
they shatter even the strength of iron
and bronze.
And when two people understand
each other
in their innermost hearts,
their words are sweet and strong,
like the fragrance of orchids.'

Confucius

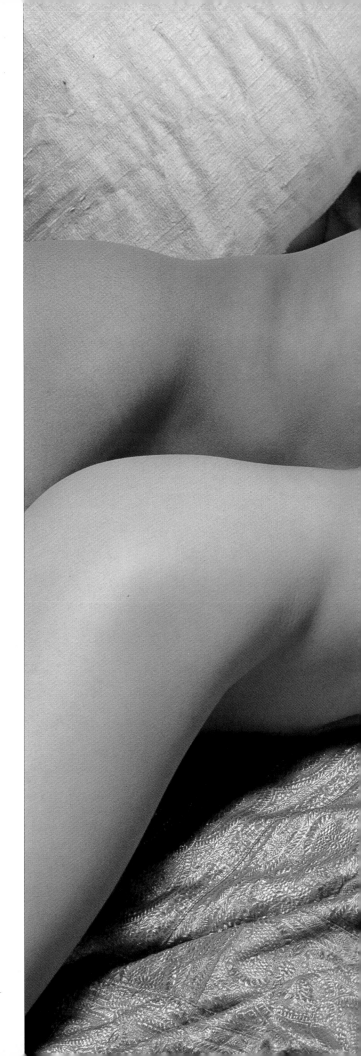

Further Reading

Anand, Margo. *The Art of Sexual Ecstasy.* New York: J P Tarcher, (hardback) 1989, (paperback) 1991.

Burton, Richard (trans.). *The Kama Sutra.* London: Guild Publishing, 1987 (and various editions).

Burton, Richard (trans.). *The Perfumed Garden.* Rochester, Vermont: Inner Traditions, 1992 (and various editions).

Chang, Jolan. *The Tao of Love and Sex.* London: Panther, 1977; New York: Viking Penguin, 1991.

Chia, Mantak. *Healing Love Through the Tao.* Huntingdon, New York: Healing Tao Books, 1987.

Chopel, Gedun (translated by Hopkins, Jeffrey). *Tibetan Arts of Love.* New York: Snow Lion Publications, 1992.

Douglas, Nik and Slinger, Penny. *Sexual Secrets.* Rochester, Vermont: Destiny Books 1979 (Inner Traditions, 1992).

Freke, Timothy (edited by Palmer, Martin). *Lao Tzu's Tao Te Ching.* London: Piatkus, 1995.

Russell, Stephen and Kolb, Jurgen. *The Tao of Sexual Massage.* New York: Simon & Schuster, 1992.

Sadi (translated by Rehatsek, Edward). *The Rose Garden.* Victoria, Australia: New Humanity Books, 1990.

Wildwood, Chrissie. *Erotic Aromatherapy.* New York: Sterling Publishing Co., 1994.

Index

Page numbers in *italics* refer to illustrations

Acknowledgements

I could not have written this book without the critical eye and practical support of my lover Victoria Moseley. Thank you for sharing your heart with me. I am also deeply grateful to my agent Susan Mears, my consultant Yvette Mayo, the friendly and professional team at Eddison Sadd, the beautiful models, talented photographers, and all the wonderful people who made this book what it is. May the omnipresent power of love fill your lives.

Eddison Sadd would like to thank the following for the loan of props:

Alternative East
48 Upper Street
Islington
London N1 0PN
Tel. 0171 226 9504
Metallic embroidered drapes and cushion covers featured in chapters two, four, six, seven and nine.

Diva
23/24 Upper Street
Islington
London N1 0PQ
Tel. 0171 359 3539
Coloured glass bottles used throughout book.

Rau
36 Islington Green
Islington
London N1 8DU
Tel. 0171 359 5337
Kilim rug, purple and gold sari and pink bolster covers featured in chapters one, three, five and eight, and brass bowls, carved wooden table, metal beakers, fruit bowl, brass ewer featured on page 8.

Thanks also to Pritty Ramjee for selected props.

EDDISON·SADD EDITIONS

Project Editor	Zoë Hughes
Copy-editor	Vivienne Wells
Proof-reader	Pat Pierce
Indexer	Dorothy Frame
Art Director	Elaine Partington
Senior Art Editor	Sarah Howerd
Mac Designer	Brazzle Atkins
Illustrator	Alan McGowan
Photographers	Alistair Hughes, Howard Allman and Barry Chandler
Production	Charles James